The Invergordon Smelter
A Case Study in Management

The Invergordon Smelter
A Case Study in Management

G. Gordon Drummond

Hutchinson Benham, London

Hutchinson Benham Limited
3 Fitzroy Square, London W1

An imprint of the Hutchinson Group

London Melbourne Sydney Auckland
Wellington Johannesburg and agencies
throughout the world

First published 1977
© British Aluminium Company Ltd 1977

Set in Monotype Times

Printed in Great Britain by
The Anchor Press Ltd, and bound by
Wm Brendon & Son Ltd, both of
Tiptree, Essex

ISBN 0 09 129871 7

Contents

Foreword

by PROFESSOR K. J. W. ALEXANDER
Chairman of the Highlands and Islands Development Board

We have here a fascinating piece of recent industrial history, a case study of a major element in the regeneration of the economic life of the highlands and islands, and a manual for managers and others confronted with the daunting task of taking a major investment decision through to successful production on a green field site far from the main centres of industrial activity. This latter aspect is the most original of the author's contributions, and there is no doubt that he has successfully filled an important gap in management literature.

The significance for highland prospects of Gordon Drummond's achievement in establishing the smelter at Invergordon and the fact that he has now joined the Highlands and Islands Development Board as a full-time member able to devote his talents to a wider range of development possibilities and projects would be sufficient reason for me to welcome this book, but its wider implications for management education and for industrial policy reinforces my pleasure in congratulating the author and commending his book.

May 1977

1 Inception and Preparation

On 24 July 1968 the President of the Board of Trade announced in the House of Commons that Government approval had been given for the proposal by The British Aluminium Company Ltd to build a £37 million aluminium smelter at Invergordon, Ross and Cromarty. This marked the culmination of several years of planning and negotiation by British Aluminium, Alcan and Rio Tinto Zinc for the establishment of three new smelters constituting a large addition to the United Kingdom aluminium industry.

Hitherto the aluminium industry in Great Britain had been largely concerned with the production of sheet, strip, tube, section and foil and castings. It was only to be expected that attention should focus on the design and construction of three new production units capable of adding 260000 tons a year of primary (i.e. unwrought) aluminium to UK smelting capacity hitherto limited to a figure of nearly 40000 tons annual capacity at the Highland Reduction Works of British Aluminium.

Construction of the plants at Invergordon, Lynemouth and Anglesey began in the autumn of 1968 and considerable publicity attended progress on all three sites. But less attention was given to the concomitant preparations for operation of the smelters by their permanent staffs.

Beginning in early 1969, the nuclei of the eventual operating managements were created by all three of the companies concerned. It is significant that in each of the three projects these moves took place at the same time, indicating similarity of outlook on the tasks involved and the period of gestation required of an organization capable of operating a smelter to specific levels of performance and to a particular timetable.

In the case of the British Aluminium smelter, an engineering design and procurement group was set up at the Southall, West London, office of Taywood Wrightson Ltd, a consortium arranged for the purpose, while initial earth-moving and foundation work got under way on site at Inverbreakie Farm just outside Invergordon in the County of Ross and Cromarty, some 600 miles north. The nucleus operating group occupied a desk and two chairs in an otherwise empty office overlooking St James's Square, London (a mere few hundred yards from one of its competitors) in January 1969. This location within head office of BA gave easy access to the design team at Southall, was convenient for mounting the extensive programme of consultation and visitation abroad which quickly ensued, and yet was not inconvenient for site meetings. This choice displayed the distinctly different nature of the task facing the operating team by comparison with that of the design team. The work consisted largely of manpower and logistical studies which involved closer contact with BA central personnel, financial and related departments than with design and construction and engineering activities.

It was clear that no attempt should be made to become too closely involved in the work of the design team. Regular contact was established to ensure involvement in key decisions on a highly selective basis. This dichotomy may seem surprising given the importance of process parameters in determining optimum levels of manning and methods of control, but it made for clear understanding of the separate responsibilities of the two teams and enabled decisions to be made in the light of contrasting interests.

The first task undertaken by the operating team nucleus was a trip to study organizational structure and manning levels at four comparable smelters in the USA. No attempt was made on this trip to investigate numerous other relevant operational aspects of these plants except to gather performance reports and statistical details of process variations as well as product mix. It was evident from analysis of visit reports that, in spite of local organizational variants, there were two principal operational activities, viz. process operation and plant maintenance – both supported in turn by the usual service functions of accounting, personnel, quality control and various kinds of resource measurement. Having obtained this information, the first organizational structure design for Invergordon was drafted in April 1969. This provided for division into six main functions, viz. production, engineering, technical, industrial engineering, personnel and accounting. This division proposed the placing of like activities together.

At this stage it was decided to set down and adopt a glossary of standard terms to replace the several terms in common use for various organizational and process features. This facilitated clarification of authority levels. Later on it was found to be of advantage in defining communications practice, as in briefing meetings or grievance procedure.

Having regard to the distribution of cost between consumption of materials and wages bill, it was evident, even at the feasibility study stage, that the new smelter would show a high process-material cost largely attributable to the heavy power consumption inseparable from the electrolytic reduction process used to reduce aluminium oxide (alumina) to metal. Other process materials, such as alumina itself, petroleum coke and chemical fluxes, form major expense items; but the critical factor in aluminium smelter operation is the ability to use electrical power efficiently. For this reason the organization disposition, motivation and control of manpower is of the greatest significance in economic terms as it affects the consumption of power. This is not to say that productivity *per se*, i.e. the expression of productive efficiency in terms of man hours a tonne, could be regarded as unimportant in itself in a plant whose wages bill would amount to some £¾ million a year at full capacity. But the vital factor was seen to be the ability so to mobilize manpower resources as to achieve effective response to variations in process control parameters initiated by the plant management. The alumina reduction process was regarded as capable of being regulated by production supervision within prescribed conditions and limits, with deviation from normal conditions being met by some new or revised prescription. In other words, the task of the production function was to operate the processes by careful supervision of the operating personnel while the task of the technical function was to monitor process control and to prescribe problem remedies and, of course, introduce new techniques as process conditions are changed.

For these reasons, a short chain of communication from management to operator was essential in all departments with a shallow hierarchical tree. In fact, an operator/supervisor ratio of 5:6:1 eventuated. The overall ratio of hourly-paid to salaried staff in 1972 was 1:58:1.

The summer and autumn of 1969 were taken up with detailed study of unit operations comparable to those then being worked up by the design team from which manpower studies evolved leading to the promulgation of the first edition of the Manpower Schedule in April 1970. This document comprised:

1 Summary of planned department complements.
2 Organization charts for all departments.
3 Summary of overall recruitment programme.
4 Monthly programme of jobs to be filled.
5 Programme of monthly departmental intake.

Not only did this document lay down in explicit detail the planned organization of every function, department, shift, section and individual job, but it served as a basic communications and budgeting tool. From this point onwards the approved manpower schedule acted as the basic working plan for the embryonic personnel function which began to form in 1970.

With the objectives of low cost operation of a capital intensive undertaking, it was obvious that appropriate working conditions must be devised which would relate to Invergordon in its infancy and which would enable further development to take place throughout the projected life of the plant. A far-sighted policy decision at board level enabled planning for Invergordon to proceed on a basis of 'non-comparability', i.e. that proposals would be formulated on the basis of relevance to Invergordon's needs rather than to precedents obtained elsewhere. As a result, detailed study of industry-wide practices led to the conclusion of an agreement with the National Union of General and Municipal Workers and the Electrical and Electronics Trade Union/Plumbers Trade Union in December of the same year. These agreements gave expression to the view that high manpower utilization and motivation could only be achieved through:

1 Clear objective setting.
2 Careful personnel recruitment.
3 Effective training.
4 Effective man management.

and implied formal definition and recognition of employee representation in all matters, but especially wages and conditions of employment, grievance procedures, disciplinary procedures and consultative procedures.

It had been recognized from the beginning that a formidable

task lay ahead in the field of training. As a result, the Industrial Training Service was invited to provide an instructional and consultative resource for the duration of the setting-up phase of the project. A feature of the process which then evolved within the growing operating management team under the guidance of ITS was the central belief in the importance of each job being defined and analysed by the immediate supervisor with a view to each recruit being wholly trained by his own supervisor. This involved training the supervisors in the techniques of instruction and was ultimately carried into practice in each section as it was formed in 1970–71.

By mid-1970, personnel practices for selection of personnel for all job categories had been completed and recruitment was a major activity through the autumn of 1970 and the ensuing winter. It was found that approximately nine applications must be reviewed in order to find three candidates regarded as suitable for interview, from which one was likely to be selected.

The interview system was thorough, comprising a personal history interview, industrial relations interview, medical examination, aptitude-test session and, finally, personal interview of the applicant by his prospective supervisor. The collated results of all five interviews of each applicant were considered by a review panel consisting of all interviewing personnel plus two representatives of senior management. This intensive effort took many weeks to complete at the rate of sixteen applicant interviews a day, but commissioning of the first reduction cells began on 1 May 1971, with all complements full and trained.

The above account outlines the approach adopted for the task of organization, design and creation. Succeeding chapters give fuller descriptions of the way in which each aspect was actually tackled.

2 Construction of the Smelter

The organization of construction

Before any return on the huge investments being committed could begin to flow, the smelter and its supporting facilities, the pier for intake of raw materials, the reinforcement of the electricity power grid, the water supply, had all to be designed and constructed. In the case of the smelter itself, this task was entrusted to a consortium formed for the purpose by two well-known firms. The firms were Taylor Woodrow (Construction) Ltd and Head Wrightson Ltd, experienced respectively in civil and mechanical and electrical engineering with long histories of involvement in major projects at home and overseas. While the direction of the Invergordon project was to remain securely in the hands of British Aluminium, it was decided that execution of directions from BA was to be vested in the consortium to be known as Taywood Wrightson Ltd. A small team of senior project engineers was drawn from Reynolds Metals Company (the minority parent shareholder in BA) and BA itself for the purpose of issuing directives to the Taywood Wrightson (TWW) organization as to policy, parameters and, of course, to exercise both positive and negative controls over all aspects of design, material procurement, construction and commissioning of the smelter.

This approach was not yet universal, or even common, in Britain in 1969 but, in view of the implications, it is worth explaining why this particular method of project management was adopted. There were several alternative approaches, each with its influential and articulate advocates, and these included:

1 Direct management by BA.
2 Management through professional architects and consultancy engineers.
3 A mixture of 1 and 2.
4 An arm's-length turnkey management contract to be placed

with one of several major firms already engaged in the aluminium industry.

The approach adopted was to place a package-deal management contract with TWW, vesting in that organization responsibility for design, procurement, construction and commission of the smelter to a definitive specification, cost estimate and completion programme. The reasons for the adoption of this particular course were:

1 The ability which it offered to the client to monitor, supervise (and intervene if necessary) and control activity and progress in all respects without the involvement of scarce, heavily-committed technical resources – performance to be controlled with reference to a single coordinating plan comprising all elements in the project.

2 The ability to specify and adopt uniformity in technical and commercial practices in the field of material procurement with the advantages which this was expected to offer of better control of quality and delivery, purchasing power strength and significant cost savings, to which must be added the benefits during construction and subsequent operation of standardization in electrical and other common equipment units.

3 The ability to exercise a better control over industrial relations on a site where a variety of contractors would be employing up to 2000 men and hence promote both productivity and stability.

4 The enhanced ability of the client to hold a single management agency fully accountable for its performance.

5 The elimination of discontinuities in design and actual construction with consequential benefits in materials flow, eventual process control and the saving of time in construction.

6 The clear opportunity to reduce aggregate overheads – especially on site – in the construction phase.

In the above respects it was believed that the method adopted offered real advantages which would be valuable in real terms and which would not be easy to achieve – if indeed they were even possible to achieve by any of the other methods.

A number of consortia made overtures to BA. TWW had a number of powerful competitors but it was chosen because of its competitive offer and the impressive resources which it could demonstrate were immediately available. The relevance of all this to the eventual operating capability lay, in 1969–70, in the clear delineation of responsibilities and authorities which flowed from its adoption with the consequent ease of cross-referencing ability which ensued. Later on, in the outcome, there emerged the advantage of successful completion and discharge by TWW of its obligations in completion of construction on time and within budget. This was, and still is, a rare claim to be made for any British construction project, but there was the disadvantage of the inevitable – almost constitutional – weakness in the commissioning stage. So one serious criticism could be advanced that the elimination of a number of small and perhaps short-lived interfaces was achieved at the price of a much more serious interface with longer-term implications for the operating management. By any standards, this was a well conceived and executed construction project. However, the full exposition of how that was achieved belongs to another book.

Ancillary facilities

Of course, while TWW were engaged in Southall and on the former farm of Inverbreakie just north of the burgh of Invergordon, a 3300-foot-long pier was being designed by consulting engineers Babtie, Shaw and Morton to meet BA's requirements and was built in the Cromarty Firth by Edmund Nuttall Ltd in less than two years, being completed early in 1971 on time and within budget. The provision of the residential camp was in the hands of TWW, but the North of Scotland Hydro-Electric Board (NOSHEB) had important reinforcing work to carry out on the national power grid in order to be albe to supply power to the smelter. Aluminium smelters have a large appetite for electric power which, in the case of Invergordon, amounted to 189 MW in the first instance, later increased within the provisions of the agreement negotiated between NOSHEB and BA to 200 MW – a quantity equivalent to that required by a city of 180000 inhabitants (such as Aberdeen or Dundee). Additional services were also required before the smelter could begin to operate. Most of these fell within the province of one or other of the various public authorities. Here lay an interesting problem: how to ensure that all the services, such as water and telecommunications, infrastucture such as houses and schools, not to mention roads and sewerage and, importantly, the improvement of recreational facilities, would be provided. With very commendable foresight and imagination, a special organization was called into being by the Scottish Development Department charged with the oversight and coordination of the planning and execution of the provision of all these services and facilities. How this was done deserves description here.

The Invergordon Steering Group

The decision by the Government to sanction the building of new aluminium smelters was based on wider considerations of policy than those relating to regional development alone. Therefore it was important that the projects should, in all respects, be successful. The Highlands of Scotland had been the seat of peculiarly intractable problems in the way of reviving depressed communities and a sagging economy whose decay had continued for some 200 years. Having established the Highlands and Islands Development Board and created strong financial incentives for development in regions such as the Highlands, it was to be hoped that, when an opportunity arrived to take a major step forward, its launching and execution would be characterized by the energy and imagination which the occasion deserved and, indeed, demanded. Happily the Scottish Office rose to the occasion in fostering the unprecedented creation of a Steering Group. This consisted of representatives of all interested parties for jointly planning and overseeing the provision of houses, schools, water and drainage supplies and so on to support the industrial development in Easter Ross of which the smelter was the forerunner. The earlier arrival of the largest grain distillery in Europe at Invergordon took place in the same area at a time when manpower was already available following the rundown of the naval dockyard some time before.

In September 1968 the formation of the Steering Group was announced and its first meeting was held in Dingwall on 19 September 1968. At the outset three main problems were identified:

1 The coordination and progress control of contracts simultaneously under execution in Easter Ross (other than that for construction of the smelter itself).

2 The impact of the labour force involved in these activities on local resources.

3 The provision of social amenities, health and welfare services for the new population during the construction period and thereafter.

In addition, it was recognized that, if all the various works were to come to fruition at the same time, there must be appropriate management capability. There should also be coordination to avoid the frustrating effects of competition for the same scarce resources. It was envisaged that it would be advantageous to employ a specialist firm to provide the necessary management services for planning, progress control and expediting activities. The importance of viewing all the related activities as forming part of a single endeavour was central to this administrative concept and bore an attractive comparison to the pattern which events were taking – the formation of a new community. As past experience of major developments in essentially rural areas had not been wholly encouraging it was believed that a coordinating body should be formed. It was arranged that the Invergordon Steering Group would consist of representatives of the County Council, the Town Council of Invergordon, the Highlands and Islands Development Board (HIDB) and the Scottish Development Department, together with a representative of any major industrial developer. The Steering Group was constituted from members or officials with authority to speak for their respective interests and acted as both a consultative forum and as a management board for the entire non-industrial undertaking, using Taylor Woodrow (Management Consultants) Ltd as the executive arm of the Steering Group.

During its three-year life, the Steering Group met on twenty-five occasions, at first at regular monthly intervals, with the frequency diminishing as the various sub-projects were completed on schedule. In that time the group was able to fulfil the expectations and hopes of its foster-parents. Problems, ranging from delays in site work due to weather or shortage of materials to the apparent unawareness of the nature and importance of the developments on the part of important public and private agencies, were all solved. Sometimes this was possible because the progress reports showing actual – against planned – progress increasingly prompted corrective action. But there were other occasions when the spur of prospective exposure in front of the group led to last-ditch efforts preventing both embarrassment and, much worse, failure to accomplish. Seldom, but signally, there was the stimulus of interrogation and, now and again, conflicts of interest were resolved by sheer confrontation.

Time-consuming and expensive it may have been from the direct cost standpoint, a political hot potato it can scarcely have been in truth, but a driving force the Invergordon steering group certainly was; and, best of all, it was effective and undeniably successful.

The Highlands and Islands Development Board

This Board was set up in 1965 under the Highlands and Islands Development (Scotland) Act 1965. In this event may be seen the culmination of the efforts and recommendations of many individuals, committees, commissions, working parties, study groups and so on which had been studying the problems of the Highlands of Scotland over many years.

These problems included decreasing population and a persistently higher average rate of unemployment than for Scotland as a whole in spite of substantial Government expenditure in one form or another. A number of agencies charged with revitalizing the economy of the Highlands had been at work, and prominent among these were the North of Scotland Hydro-Electric Board, the Forestry Commission, the Crofters Commission and the Scottish Tourish Board in addition to the powers and responsibilities exercised by central and local government. In spite of all these bodies and their efforts and the especially noteworthy work of the Highlands and Islands Advisory Panel, it was increasingly evident that there was a clamant need for coordination and grouping of incentives and efforts if any regional development policy was to be successful in reversing the steadily increasing debilitation evident in the Highlands and Islands. Thus it was that when the Development Board was set up in 1965, this event received general acclaim.

Section 1 of the Act lays down that

For the purpose of assisting the people of the Highlands and Islands to improve their economic and social conditions and of enabling the Highlands and Islands to play a more effective part in the economic and social development of the nation, there shall be established a Highlands and Islands Development Board which shall have the general function of preparing, concerting, promoting, assisting and undertaking measures for the economic and social development of the Highlands and Islands.

Early in its life it came to believe in the need to achieve substantial progress which would be regarded as evidence of real accomplishment in the eyes of the public and of potential developers. To do so would be difficult enough in any location but less difficult if the concept of growth-point concentration were to prove practicable. It was argued that selected centres of industrial development would prove to be natural foci of industrial development if only this could be shown to work in practice. With the United Kingdom Atomic Energy Authority establishment at Dounreay, the Wiggins-Teape pulp and paper mill at Fort William and the new distillery at Invergordon, this view was obviously plausible. The Board deserves credit for identifying a strategy for industrial development of the Highlands and Islands before North Sea oil was discovered. The policy was studied, enunciated and pursued energetically and with a certain panache. As a result, the possibilities of industrial development on the shores of the Cromarty Firth allied to and even determined by the availability of flat land close to a safe harbour with ample deep water were recognized. Included in these possibilities was the siting of an aluminium smelter near Invergordon. While the matter soon became embroiled in controversy by reason of the interest of the aluminium industry and central government in bringing about a major increase in the primary aluminium production capacity of Britain, the HIDB had rightly foreseen that the Invergordon site was one of the most advantageous in a relatively short list of locations suitable for such smelters in Britain. Throughout the debate on the various issues raised in the course of securing planning consent under the Town and Country Planning Act, the HIDB played a distinctly positive role in arguing the matter, just as it contributed a similarly positive influence to the proceedings of the Invergordon steering group.

The County Council of Ross and Cromarty

The local authority responsible for the development of Easter Ross was the County Council of Ross and Cromarty, a council whose powers extended over a total area of 3089 square miles stretching from the Moray Firth, leading out to the North Sea in the east, to the shores of Wester Ross, bordering on the North Minch. This was mountainous, sparsely populated land supporting hill-farming, forestry and tourism as its main industries. The resources of the County Council were necessarily spread thinly in attempting to serve scattered small communities. For long enough the population had been shrinking in spite of the magnificent surroundings, for life was hard on the hill farms and crofts, and also in spite of the pioneering work of NOSHEB in bringing electric power to the glens.

Easter Ross, as the territory east of Dingwall in the county area is known, differs in many respects from the rest of the county. The land is relatively flat and much of it has been well farmed by a community enjoying fertile soil and temperate weather. But even in the east, increasing costs brought increasing mechanization to the farms with a resultant fall in the numbers employed in agriculture. There was little industry and in 1956 the naval establishment at Invergordon was reduced to the operation of the oil storage depot and intermittent use of the depot pier in which only fifty men were employed. During two world wars, the Invergordon naval base had been the focus of much activity, bringing trade and employment to the town, and now this had gone. It was with enthusiasm and relief that the town welcomed the Invergordon Distillery Company, a major new development which arrived in 1962 and was employing 360 people by 1965. However, this level could not be sustained and, by 1967, the numbers at work in the distillery had fallen to 160.

The economy of the county had been experiencing progressive decline for many years in common with the rest of the Highlands and, if the HIDB had been set up to reverse the trend, Ross and Cromarty County Council was sufficiently concerned by the state of affairs to resolve upon a policy of industrial development. This was formally agreed at a meeting of the Council on 6 December 1967 and, under the Convener, the Rev. Murdo Nicolson, supported by the County Clerk, Mr J. M. Dunlop, the County Council embarked on a policy of self-help and began to promote the advantages and opportunities which it possessed. Development staff were recruited and put to work; the Jack Holmes group was jointly commissioned with the HIDB to prepare a comprehensive development strategy. Other ventures were also set in motion.

While this was going on, the aluminium industry was reflecting on the fact that, with the advent of nuclear power, it was now possible to site smelters on any location rather than close to large hydro-electric power resources as before. Again, the major firms in the industry had their own particular motives for examining in detail the possibilities for smelter development in Britain. Surveys of possible sites produced an interesting unanimity in the short list of choices. While RTZ favoured North Wales, BA and Alcan both selected Invergordon as first preference.

The choice of Invergordon was not difficult to make but, for the County Council, statutory planning requirements insisted that development must take place on land which had been designated for the appropriate purpose. Each planning authority, as defined by the Town and Country Planning Act, is required to produce a development plan for its own area in which land is zoned for industrial development, agriculture, housing or for whatever purpose might be foreseen in the future. In the case of the Invergordon area, much of the land suitable for industrial development was good farming land and, in pursuit of its development policy, it was necessary for the County Council as planning authority to re-zone the land and gain approval for its proposals from the Secretary of State for Scotland. To this end, proposals were published for the smelter development and, because of the objections lodged by the opponents of development, a public inquiry was necessary and this opened in Dingwall on 27 February 1968. Evidence was led by the County Council, by the developers and by the objectors and the Reporter submitted his findings to the Secretary of State who approved Amendment No. 3 to the County Development Plan on 5 June 1968.

The role of the County Council in its capacity as planning authority was complemented by its other roles in different spheres – education, housing, roads and so on. In all of these, the Council determined policy and its full-time staff of officials translated policy into action results which were compatible because of the comprehensive unity of the Council's development strategy. While this Council was not constitutionally different from any other in Scotland, it was distinctly more enterprising and energetic than most others. More important, it had decided on its objective – the achievement of a healthy and prosperous society through economic development – decided on the strategic approach and then proceeded to execution. Thus the County Council and British Aluminium were able to form an effective and happy relationship because of the virtually complete compatibility of their interests and because both worked hard at implementation of their plans each with an ear cocked to the voice of the other.

The attitude of The British Aluminium Company

The British Aluminium Company began operations in the Highlands of Scotland in 1896. At Foyers in Inverness-shire on the shores of Loch Ness, the young company started the very first reduction works in Great Britain. The works drew on hydro-electric power from a catchment area of 100 square miles in Stratherrick and continued in operation, latterly in the production of super-purity aluminium, until 1966. Later, in 1907, a larger factory came into operation at Kinlochleven, Argyll, and again in 1929 an even larger factory began just outside Fort William, Inverness-shire. These two plants have been operating successfully ever since and still enjoy an important place in the company's production capability. Thus BA has been in the Highlands since the late nineteenth century, is a major landowner and a major employer (and a major ratepayer) and, as such, is an established feature of the Highland scene. In economic terms, there can be no argument that the company's activities have not been very beneficial. Indeed, and equally, BA not only has learnt what is involved in operating factories in the North of Scotland but is, in itself, a part of Highland society.

Thus the planning of a fourth, even larger, development of its aluminium reduction resources at Invergordon – only thirty-two miles as the crow flies from Foyers – seemed to many of its employees something like a dream about to come true. If not a dream about to come true, it was certainly the event of a lifetime and so exercised a magnetic appeal to the imagination and aspirations. But any temptation to glamorize the impending development was not hard to resist in view of what lay ahead. The start-up of a big new smelter is no picnic and no place for starry-eyed enthusiasts. Enthusiasm was, of course, essential but it had to be tempered with sober realism in the face of the long hours of work, the accidents and failures that would inevitably occur. Just as the planning and design of the hardware demanded a deliberate, very calculating approach as did the approach to the software and in-plant personnel policy, this applied equally to the introduction of the company and its new project to the residents of Easter Ross. This introduction was considered and developed with premeditation. After due thought, a policy statement was produced and circulated within the company, then to the outside audience. The statement was distributed to all those in BA involved in the Invergordon project and presented line-by-line to operating staff so that there could be no mistaking the intention. The presentation may not have been subtle or even effective but put across it was, as follows:

B.A. AT INVERGORDON
AN EXPRESSION OF POLICY

British Aluminium's investment in a reduction works at Invergordon is setting in motion major economic and social changes in the Highlands. Although the company has no control or influence over many of the changes taking place, it is alert to its responsibilities as prime mover.

As elsewhere, the company intends to be a good neighbour, a fair employer and a worthy corporate member of the community. This means that in all its activities, both during the construction period and after the plant is in operation, BA must consider the effect of its actions on others.

The company also accepts that the people of the surrounding area expect to be told what is going on in their midst and to be treated with the consideration due to the established inhabitants of a place where BA is the newcomer.

It is the duty of every BA employee concerned with the smelter development to remember this company attitude in his dealings with the people and the organisations of the area, and to endeavour to foster an understanding of BA's approach among the staff of outside concerns working for the company.

BA will be judged by its actions – and those of the contractors and others serving it – and also by what is known of those actions and the reasons for them. The judgement of the people of Invergordon and the surrounding region, individually and collectively, will shape BA's reputation for the future.

Early in 1969 began an extensive but carefully modulated programme of community relations. This was designed to introduce the company through leading personalities, to describe and explain its plans and their implications as these became known, to inform as many people as possible of continuous developments (before they occurred if likely to be unwelcome), by public meetings, press releases and constant contact with local government councillors and officials, press and television.

To publish an explicit statement of policy is one thing. To put it into practice is something else. As the policy statement foresaw, history is the best judge, so let the record speak for itself. Confirmation of the decision to proceed was finally announced at a press conference in which the chairman of The British Aluminium Company Ltd, Sir William Strath, KCB (himself a Scotsman), was joined by the chairman of the Highlands and Islands Development Board, Sir Robert Grieve, and Mr R. E. Utiger, managing director of British Aluminium, among others. The press conference was held in Inverness and was given widespread coverage by local and national press and television. Soon afterwards Mr Utiger chaired a public meeting in Invergordon Town Hall, attended by 500 people (150 being turned away), at which the main implications of the project for local residents were explained. Also present were Canon McHardy, Provost of Invergordon, and Mr Alfred Smith, Director of Personnel for BA. A significant move had occurred in August 1968 when Mr J. C. Munro was appointed as BA site representative at Inverbreakie Farm – a happy choice in that an experienced reduction superintendent bearing a surname prominent in Easter Ross should have a gift for the ice-breaking role of introducing BA as a presence in the local community. BA had a caravan at the Invergordon Highland Games, held as usual at Rosskeen, in August 1968. In charge of the caravan were Mr Pat Bowman and Mr Jimmy More. Pat was Press and Public Relations Officer from BA head office in London while Jimmy had only recently retired from a long and innovative career as a senior engineer with BA at Kinlochleven and Lochaber. The caravan was a centre of attraction for visitors to the games who were able to see a three-dimensional scale model of the smelter.

But, of course, the story of the introduction of the British Aluminium Company as developer in Easter Ross to the public and to those closely interested had begun some considerable time before.

In November 1967, a party of journalists from the national

press was taken to visit the Kinlochleven, Lochaber and Falkirk factories and, in February 1968, the managing director of BA at the time, Mr G. B. Margraf, with other BA executives visited the HIDB, Ross and Cromarty County Council and Invergordon Burgh Council.

During the public inquiry in Dingwall in March 1968, extensive personal contacts were established with Highland press, radio and TV representatives by British Aluminium's PRO, Pat Bowman, with whom the fourth estate was to develop an intimate and trusting association. Next came a press conference to mark the start of construction, mailing of a letter from the managing director of BA to 20000 homes, distribution of basic education material from the Aluminium Federation to all schools in Easter Ross and circulation of *The BA News* (the company house magazine) to selected councillors and others in the Invergordon area.

October 1968 saw 'What's Happening at Invergordon', a give-away leaflet produced for distribution through the burgh office, employment exchange, hotels and banks to answer basic public and visitors' questions.

There followed briefing meetings and visits for local councillors and officials, including a trip to BA head office and to the project design team based at TWW headquarters in Southall; the publication of a bulletin in October 1969 reporting progress on site to the local population; frequent press and TV site visits and press conferences. Of course, attention was also attracted by the succession of VIPs who made their way to Inverbreakie, beginning with the Secretary of State for Scotland, Mr William Ross, MBE, MP, in September 1968 and including Mr Edward Heath, MP, and others.

But much more important was the attempt to inform people living in the areas in and around Invergordon of impending development before the events. Residents (many of whom were retired) of Saltburn village, immediately to the east of Invergordon, were told of the details of building the new pier at a public meeting by representatives of Edmund Nuttall, pier contractors, and Babtie, Shaw and Morton, consulting engineers, and were thereby warned in advance of blasting and pile-driving activities. Similarly, queries and complaints were treated as carefully and sympathetically as possible. Wear and tear on roads between quarries and Inverbreakie caused by contractors' heavy vehicles was the subject of criticism and complaint, leading to road repairs being carried out by TWW to the satisfaction of the local authority highway engineers. The construction camp providing residential facilities for site workers was well-equipped with barber-shop, post office, TV lounge and bar and firmly managed by TWW. Many clubs and societies invited speakers from BA and TWW to describe the smelter and its implications for them; explanatory leaflets and brochures were widely circulated.

This account does no more than sample the extensive campaign of activities carefully organized and controlled by BA in the implementation of its policy statement. While there was no expectation that those opposed to industrial development would be converted to a different point of view, it was hoped that the objection might be diminished and that some basis of reconciliation or *modus vivendi* might be found.

At the end of 1971, with the construction phase completed, a new phase began. By 1972 it was reasonable to believe that the smelter had become an established feature of the local social and topographical landscape.

3 The Aluminium Industry

The case for investment

Various reasons have been adduced from time to time as to the reasons for the decision by British Aluminium to build a large aluminium smelter in 1967 and, in particular, for choosing to do so at Invergordon. As was made clear by the President of the Board of Trade in his statement in July 1968, the Government was sympathetic to the proposals by RTZ and British Aluminium. Not only would the proposals bring into being very substantial industrial developments but the importing of relatively cheap raw materials in place of the more expensive products improved the balance of export/import payments of the British economy.

The Ministerial announcement was as follows:

Aluminium Smelters

The President of the Board of Trade (Mr Anthony Crosland):
  With permission, I wish to make a statement on aluminium smelters.
  I informed the House on 10th July that Alcan Aluminium (UK) Limited was proceeding with a smelter in Northumberland. The Board of Trade and the generating boards have now reached agreement with the British Aluminium Company and the RTZ/BICC consortium on the major outstanding questions relating to their smelter projects. The companies will announce today their decisions to proceed with their smelters at Invergordon and Holyhead respectively, for both of which outline planning permission has been granted by the appropriate authorities. The arrangements are inevitably complicated, but I thought it right to inform the House immediately of their broad outlines.
  The smelters will draw power from the generating boards under special long-term contracts based on the principles announced by the Government last autumn. The companies will pay an operating charge and also a capital payment in return for which nuclear power generating capacity of the most advanced type will be earmarked to supply their requirements. My right hon. Friend, the Minister of Technology will

arrange, subject to Parliamentary approval, to buy from the companies their rights in the relevant share of the plutonium arising in the nuclear reactors; the plutonium will thus remain under Government control.

The Board of Trade has agreed, subject to the approval of Parliament, to make loans to the companies at an interest rate of 7 per cent under the Industrial Expansion Act. These loans, which will be of up to £29 million in the case of British Aluminium and £33 million in the case of RTZ, will be the subject of industrial investment schemes under that Act. They will be equal in amount to the capital contributions required by the generating boards. The necessary schemes, and a fuller statement will be laid before Parliament in the autumn.

These two new smelters will each have an initial capacity of 100000 tons per annum. This, together with the first 60000 ton stage of the new Alcan smelter at Lynemouth, will provide a total new United Kingdom capacity of 260000 tons per annum. All three companies have agreed to consult the Government before extending their capacity further.

I have informed the Norwegian and other EFTA Governments, and also the Canadian and US Governments, with all of whom we have had a full exchange of views, of these decisions.

SIR K. JOSEPH

How long is it since Rio Tinto first proposed an aluminium smelter scheme to the Government? How many jobs, excluding construction, are expected to be created at Invergordon and Holyhead respectively? What is the cost of the power that the smelters will be using under the long-term contracts? Can other large continuous industrial users of energy make similar arrangements with the electricity industry?

MR CROSLAND

Of course, this has taken a long time to conclude – which is hardly surprising in view of the fact that what we are doing is, in effect, to establish an almost entirely new and very important industry – and to take decisions which involve most important regional considerations and international considerations for a new type of power contract. I make no apology for the delay which has occurred. (Hon. Members: 'How long?') I would much rather delay and have a satisfactory scheme than do what Ministers in the previous Conservative Government did – constantly rush into hasty contracts which they then had to cancel.

There will be 600 and 700 jobs approximately at Invergordon and Holyhead respectively, although the numbers employed during the construction period will probably rise to over 2000.

Details of power contracts are never made public, nor will they be in this case.

On the last point, as to other possible applicants for this type of power contract, if anyone suggests a similar type of power contract we shall consider the case on its merits in the light of the principles laid down last autumn.

MR WILLIAM HAMILTON

Can my right hon. Friend say whether his Department is satisfied that the social infrastructure – the roads, houses, schools and the rest – will be phased properly with the development of the smelter itself in Scotland? Can he say whether the time taken between the original decision of RTZ and British Alcan and now is less than the 10 years which it took the previous Conservative Administration to get on with the pulp mill?

MR CROSLAND

On the first question, yes we are satisfied that there will be the phasing my hon. Friend has in mind. On the question of the time taken, certainly it is very much less than the 10 years my hon. Friend mentioned. Since the time when the Government invited these applications it has taken nine months for what, in effect, is an entirely new industry.

MR ALASDAIR MACKENZIE

Is the President of the Board of Trade aware that his statement will give great satisfaction in Scotland, in Invergordon in particular? Is he further aware that the part played by the Scottish Office and the Highlands and Islands Development Board in bringing these protracted negotiations to a successful conclusion is very much appreciated? Further, since the Government have come to a decision, will the right hon. Gentleman do his utmost to ensure that there is an early start of the work on the project?

MR CROSLAND

I am obliged to the hon. Member for his opening remarks. I gladly join with him in paying tribute to the Scottish Office and the Highlands and Islands Development Board. On his last question, work will be started as soon as the companies find this practicable.

MR JAMES GRIFFITHS

Is my right hon. Friend aware that this news will be received with great joy in Wales? May I congratulate him on the work which has been done? Now that we are beginning to establish these new and growing industries in the old industrial areas, will my right hon. Friend do his best to persuade industrialists to establish their industries, where possible, as near to the sites of the old industries, for the need for employment there is very great?

MR CROSLAND

I am obliged to my right hon. Friend for paying tribute to the Welsh Office and its endeavours in this matter. As to the latter part of his question, a large part of the object of the entire regional policy is to attract industries and firms to the areas he has in mind.

MR NOBLE

May I add my congratulations to the President of the Board of Trade for having, perhaps rather slowly, acceded to the demands which I know he was getting from the Secretary of State for Scotland and from the Highlands and Islands Development Board? May I wish the new companies great financial success in their areas in the Highlands and in Wales?

MR MACLENNAN

Will my right hon. Friend accept that this decision will be regarded through the Highlands as a triumph and a breakthrough for industry which will lay the foundations for great benefits to come over a wide area?

MR G. CAMPBELL

Is the right hon. Gentleman aware that there will be relief in the North of Scotland that the Government have at last agreed to the site at Invergordon? Is he also aware that the reference by the hon. Member of Fife, West (Mr William Hamilton) to 10 years in relation to the pulp mill is completely incorrect? Can the right hon. Gentleman tell the House what his estimate is of when the smelter at Invergordon will be completed?

MR CROSLAND

The smelter at Invergordon will be in production by 1971. I am obliged to the hon. Member for what he said in his opening remarks, but in the light of the extreme complication of this decision I would have thought that it would evoke, particularly from the hon. Member, a rather more generous reaction.

MR J. H. OSBORN

Can the President of the Board of Trade state the price of electricity offered to the smelters, bearing in mind that the cost of electricity in other countries is very low? Can he give an assurance that there will be no need in due course for tariff protection of home smelted aluminium,

B

bearing in mind that competitors of aluminium – steel and other materials – will not have the advantages that aluminium has in this country?

MR CROSLAND
As the hon. Member must know, I cannot tell him the price. It is never revealed in contracts of this kind. I assure him, however, that it is completely unsubsidised. I can also assure him that there is no intention of imposing a tariff on aluminium imports.

MR GEOFFREY LLOYD
Was the original application by RTZ for a larger output than 100000 tons at Holyhead? If so, will the reduction to an output of 100000 tons have a bad effect in raising unit costs?

MR CROSLAND
The right hon. Gentleman is quite right in supposing that the applications from each of the three companies were for a larger capacity than we are now going ahead with in stage one. The reason why, in agreement with the companies, we reduced the capacity in stage one was to reassure our EFTA partners that we would examine any possible adverse effect on Norwegian exports to us after stage one was completed. The addition to unit costs as a result of the reduction in capacity will be very small indeed.

Hansard, 24 July 1968

But whatever the motives for the Government giving its approval to the smelter developments, the British industry had its own good reasons. These may be listed as follows:

1 The industry had a record of steady expansion and British sources of primary metal would obviously be desirable.

2 Larger, modern smelters offered advantages over older and perhaps less efficient plants overseas.

3 Given the large outputs associated with modern smelters, sources close to fabricating facilities serving the British markets would bring opportunities for closer coordination of production and demand, including that of inventory reduction with resultant financial benefits.

4 Direct control of primary metal supply is of importance in a vertically integrated industry such as aluminium manufacture.

5 Prospective entry by the United Kingdom into membership

of the European Economic Community raised questions as to the level of tariff duties likely to apply in the future regarding the commercial significance of export/import transactions as between the United Kingdom and those elements of the aluminium industry within the Community.

Other things being equal – and this involved the big assumption that adequate supplies of power would be reliably available over the life of the smelters and at commercially acceptable price levels – there were a number of significant reasons for any firm contemplating its long-term corporate plans to assure itself of a satisfactory source of primary (i.e. unwrought) aluminium to supply its British – and perhaps European – fabricating facilities and outlets.

In the case of British Aluminium, there were other attractions to be added – freedom from dependence on a partially-owned associate company in Canada, reliability of metal supplies independent of the effects of winter on the St Lawrence and the ability to coordinate output from three closely related Scottish reduction plants. All these were additionally persuasive as to the acceptability of the general proposition to build a large new smelter in Britain. Having reached this conclusion during the mid-1960s, exploratory and feasibility studies were undertaken covering about ten sites in the United Kingdom, culminating in 1967 in the choice of the Invergordon site as first preference.

Any site for a smelter must have the following characteristics:

1 Availability of large-scale power supplies.
2 Close proximity of deep-water anchorage.
3 About 500 acres of flat land with good subsoil conditions close to deep-water achorage.
4 Good road–rail transportation accessibility.
5 Adequate manpower supply.
6 Cooperative attitude of local government authorities.
7 Availability of substantial supplies of water for process purposes.

All these characteristics were shared by Invergordon and several (but not many) other sites in Great Britain. However, the choice would obviously be influenced by economic factors, principally the cost of construction of the smelter itself together with the cost of providing ancillary facilities and so-called infrastructure. In the out-turn, studies carried out by BA showed that not only was Invergordon fully acceptable in relation to the generally applicable criteria but that it would be the most economical and most predictably satisfactory site to develop. And so it transpired.

The site chosen by BA for building an aluminium reduction works (as a 'smelter' is accurately termed because the production process consists of the electrolytic reduction of aluminium oxide or alumina) lay on Inverbreakie Farm which was situated immediately to the north of the bonded warehouses belonging to the Invergordon Distillery Company. This farm was about 400 acres in extent when BA negotiated its purchase from its owner, Mr John Mann, in 1967 and, of this, 160 acres were ultimately required for the permanent smelter facilities. However, more were used during the construction phase to provide access and store equipment and materials. The land was generally flat, sloping upwards slightly to the south and easy to develop. The water table was not too near the surface and the subsoil conditions were good. No serious difficulties were envisaged in installing and operating marine, conveyor, road and rail supply transportation facilities. Deep-water anchorage was about a mile-and-a-half distant at the edge of the deep-water channel in the Cromarty Firth. Almost fifty feet of water was available at low water mean tide with good subsoil for bearing the weight of marine terminal facilities. There was no indication of the need to dredge other than for berth construction.

The NOSHEB grid system passed not far away – about five miles or so – as it linked the 132KV system to and from the hydroelectric installations at Loch Shin. An agreement had been reached for the supply of power on a 'no loss–no gain' basis (in order to preserve the Board's responsibility to protect the public interest), while British Aluminium was to receive an interest-free loan from the Government up to a total of £30 million with which it would pay for the purchase of a block of power from the new nuclear power station about to be built by the South of Scotland Electricity Board at Hunterston in Ayrshire.

The A9 trunk road from Inverness to Wick passes closes by the Burgh of Invergordon at about one mile's distance from the site. The main Inverness to Wick railway line actually passed through the corridor of land bought by BA in order that the overhead conveyor system could bring alumina from the deep-water pier into the smelter itself. Road–rail access was exceptionally good.

The supply of manpower was only too great for unemployment was rife throughout the Highlands, but especially in Invergordon where about 500 men were registered as unemployed at the Labour Exchange at the east end of the burgh. BA had considerable experience of employing Scots men and women and, far from having doubts as to the suitability of the Highland manpower for steady industrial employment, experience suggested grounds for confidence.

More than adequate water supplies could be made available from the virtually untapped reservoir at Loch Glass lying in the hills behind Evanton ready for development by the Water Board.

Finally, and one of the most important of all the relevant considerations, the attitude of all the local authorities – but especially that of the County Council of Ross and Cromarty – was most propitious. Faced with a declining economy, unemployment and no serious prospect of any major reversal of fortunes, the Council had resolved on a positive policy of promoting industrial development. The Council was not merely composed of energetic and concerned councillors but staffed by conscientious and enthusiastic officials, alive to the opportunities offered by Governmental regional development policies. BA was hopeful but anxious. Its anxieties were needless and its hopes were exceeded by the business-like reception of the Council towards a major developer of evidently serious intent, and also by the warmth of the welcome.

Why so big?

In 1967–68, the optimum size of an aluminium smelter – as defined by annual capacity in relation to (a) capital investment/ton of new capacity and (b) operating cost/ton of new capacity – was in the region of 120000 tons in plants intended to serve the international market. In special cases, such as may obtain in underdeveloped countries, smaller plants may be both economic and, in certain respects, more appropriate. At the risk of over-simplifying the options facing the investor and his design team, size is determined by the nature of the power-source, the type of reduction cell, and logistical and socio-economic considerations. Other things being equal, a new plant in the Western Hemisphere would be supplied with power from a major AC distribution system and converted on site to DC power for electrolytic purposes. Optimum performance and lowest capital investment per Kilowatt (KW) on installed rectified power capacity is obtained at about 100 Megawatt (MW) unit rating. Consequently, smelters drawing power from such sources are available in approximately 100 MW increments and the type of reduction cell predicates optimization at an installed capacity of about 200 MW. The capital cost shows economics of scale up to about 150000 tons but other considerations militate against very large plants with capacities in excess of this level. Below 100000 tons – if environmental considerations did not deserve the attention currently demanded – the Soderberg electrode type of reduction cell would offer lower capital investment advantages. Where this was combined with low cost power supplies in limited quantity, the economic prospects could still be attractive.

Since 1967–68, inflation in costs of building materials and manpower has resulted in such a steep increase in the capital investment/ton of installed capacity that it is now approaching $4000/ or approximately £2000/tonne) without significant advances in technology having as yet neen reliably established towards the achievement of reduced operating costs.

The process itself

Although aluminium was first produced by H. C. Oersted in 1825 by heating potassium amalgam with aluminium chloride to give an amalgam of aluminium and mercury which had to be separated by distillation, the metal had already been given its name as a result of earlier work by Sir Humphry Davy starting in 1807. In 1827, a further development by F. Wöhler produced the metal as a grey powder. By 1845 he was able to make metallic particles and thereby measure its specific gravity. Then Saint-Claire Deville exhibited a solid bar at the Paris Exposition of 1855, but the process now in use – and on which the vast world-wide industry has grown – was not discovered until 1886. Both Charles Martin Hall in Oberlin, Ohio, USA and Paul Louis Toussaint Héroult in France were independently investigating the electrolytic reduction of aluminium oxide to the metal itself. Hall was successful in February 1886. Simultaneously, Héroult also achieved success and filed a patent application in France in April 1886. Hall's application in the USA was not filed until July of that year. Hall's patent priority was granted when he was able to prove the date of his achievement. Héroult had to rely on the date of his patent application.

In 1888 Hall moved to Pittsburgh, Pennsylvania, where the Pittsburgh Reduction Company was formed, which in 1907 became the Aluminum Company of America.

In 1894 The British Aluminium Company Ltd was formed with Lord Kelvin as its scientific adviser and declared as its aim – 'to control as far as possible all the different portions of the process of manufacture . . . beginning with the raw material and the making of the alumina, which is afterwards converted into aluminium'. By acquiring the (British) rights for the Bayer process for the production of aluminium oxide from the mineral bauxite and the Héroult process for the reduction of alumina to aluminium, the company came into being as a pioneer at the formative stage of the aluminium industry. There were practical difficulties to be overcome at once. It was necessary to find and secure the purest possible carbon for electrode manufacture, alumina and cryolite as raw materials and cheap electric power which the reduction process used in large quantities. So it was that British Aluminium began operations, producing alumina from local bauxite at Larne Harbour, Northern Ireland, electrode carbon at Greenock and aluminium itself at Foyers on Loch Ness, using electricity generated by water power from the Falls of Foyers.

The Hall-Héroult electrolytic reduction process consists of passing electric current through molten cryolite containing alumina in solution in the course of which the alumina is reduced, liberating oxygen which combines with the anode carbon electrode to form carbon dioxide, while the molten aluminium sinks to the bottom of the electrolytic cell from which it is removed at regular intervals.

The reduction cells brought into use at Foyers in June 1896 were designed for currents of 8000 amperes. Some of the original power generating and metering equipment was in use until the plant closed in 1966. The original vertical shaft generators are almost certainly the oldest generators of this type and were among the items preserved by the NOSHEB when its large pumped storage hydro-electric scheme was opened in 1975 close to the historic site of the old reduction plant.

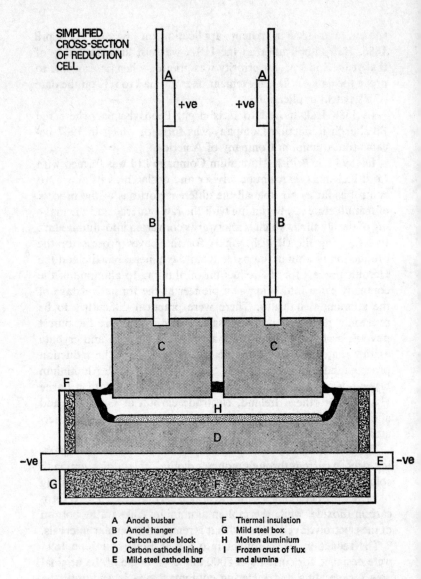

SIMPLIFIED
CROSS-SECTION
OF REDUCTION
CELL

A	Anode busbar	F	Thermal insulation
B	Anode hanger	G	Mild steel box
C	Carbon anode block	H	Molten aluminium
D	Carbon cathode lining	I	Frozen crust of flux
E	Mild steel cathode bar		and alumina

Early in the twentieth century, the market for the metal was beginning to grow and construction of a new reduction plant began in 1905 at the head of Loch Leven in Argyllshire. Operations started in December 1907 in a temporary factory which was closed when the main reduction works was started up in February 1909.

A large carbon electrode factory was built on the Kinlochleven site. This led to the closing of the small carbon factory at Greenock. From 1911 onwards, output at Kinlochleven was about 7000 tons a year, making the company's total output 8000 tons each year at a time when world output had only reached 40000 tons.

After the First World War protracted promotional activities led to the formation of the Lochaber Power Company and later the North British Aluminium Company. Work on the construction of the very large Lochaber power scheme and reduction works at Fort William, Inverness-shire began in 1924 and 2000 men were involved in the project. Twenty miles of surface railway were laid and a concrete-lined tunnel was driven from Loch Treig through Ben Nevis to Fort William, a distance of fifteen miles. By the end of 1929, the first stage had been completed and production had begun. The Lochaber hydro-electric scheme was by far the largest undertaking of its kind to be carried out in Britain and was completed in three stages. The first stage had an output of 10000 tons a year and, in 1931, the second stage was pushed ahead involving dams to raise the levels of Loch Laggan and Loch Treig and a three-mile-long tunnel to carry water between the two lochs. This stage was completed in April 1938 and added a further 10000 tons a year to BA capacity. The third stage entailed diverting flood waters from the River Spey into Loch Laggan and was completed in 1943. The Lochaber scheme raised total production capacity to well over 25000 tons a year at the time and by subsequent substantial improvements in technology and efficiency, capacity eventually reached approximately 27000 tons a year.

After the Second World War, as the demand for aluminium continued to grow, new reduction plant sites were examined in Borneo and West Africa where hydro-electric power potential existed. However, the company finally entered into partnership with the Manicouagan Power Company to build a reduction plant at Baie Comeau on the north shore of the St Lawrence in the Province of Quebec, Canada. This plant first came into operation in December 1958 and was producing approximately 100000 tons of metal a year by 1959. The partnership formed the Canadian British Aluminium Company Ltd (CBA) and, in 1968, Reynolds Metals Company of Richmond, Virginia, USA, bought the BA interest in CBA which then became known as Canadian Reynolds Metals Company (CRM).

While the Foyers cells were rated at 8000 amperes, the Kinloch-leven cells were developed in stages from current ratings of 16000 amps to 24000, 32000 and finally 40000 amps or 40 kilo-amps (KA). Lochaber began with 40 KA cells but, in post-war years, was converted to 100 KA units. By the time design work for Invergordon could begin in 1969, cells were in operation at higher current ratings and the rating chosen was 130 KA.

The extraction of alumina from bauxite

Bauxite is the ore or mineral mixture from which alumina, the oxide of the metal, is extracted in the Bayer process. It is among the most common minerals forming the crust of the earth but, of course, only those ores containing in excess of 40% alumina are mined for processing. Large deposits of bauxite are to be found in Jamaica, West Africa and North Australia but the mineral derives its name from Les Baux in the south of France where it was originally mined.

Bauxite varies widely in colour but is most commonly reddish-brown due to associated iron mineral content. It is usually mined by open-cast methods and washed and crushed for shipment to the alumina plants if they are distant. Increasingly, very large alumina plants are being located close to bauxite deposits if sufficient fossil fuel is to be found nearby for power and steam generation purposes, and a case in point is the Gove Project, of which a description is given in the paper presented by R. Furrer to the 1973 AIME conference.

Extraction of alumina begins by mixing bauxite ore with the calculated amount of alkaline liquor. The mixture is then agitated before pumping to one of a battery of kiers. These steam-jacketed vessels hold the mixture under pressure while digestion takes place over a period of about eight hours. After digestion, settling takes place and overflow liquor is filtered before decomposition to form a crystalline precipitate. Precipitated hydrated alumina is then calcined to drive off water of crystallization to form alumin.a This process is usually carried out in oil- or gas-fired rotary kilns. Extraction efficiency based on the alumina content of the bauxite should be just below 100% and, as a rule of thumb, it can be assumed that two tonnes of bauxite are required to produce one tonne of alumina. For reduction purposes, the physical characteristics of alumina are important and the two main types of electrolytic reduction cell tend to require different characteristics in the alumina used. Thus a sandy alumina is normally associated with the multi-anode cell while floury alumina is usually preferred for Soderberg cells. Sandy alumina is often coarse in terms of particle size but also dusty, forming hard crust on the electrolyte and less soluble in cryolite flux than floury aluminas.

There are two distinct kinds of alumina in use for electrolytic reduction purposes today. 'Floury' alumina is normally used in Soderberg reduction cells because it is readily soluble in cryolite flux and yet does not flow too easily when undissolved. In the side-worked Soderberg cell, alumina is fed along the side-channels where the formation of solid ridges or ledges of flux and alumina are helpful in protecting the side-lining of the cell and confining electrolytic action to the area in the 'shadow' of the anode. This kind of alumina possesses a relatively high angle-of-repose which improves sealing of the fume skirt plates thus improving fume collection efficiency and as a result, atmosphere working conditions.

The other kind of alumina is described as 'sandy' because of its texture and appearance. It is coarser than floury alumina, is dustier yet it more readily forms a hard crust above the electrolyte but is somewhat less soluble than the other kind. It does, however, flow more easily and this assists distribution so that solubility in the electrolyte may be increased but has much less tendency to form a protective ledge at the side of the reduction cell. Sandy alumina is generally used in pre-baked reduction cells, although it should be understood that the distinctions drawn above are crude and as with other materials, specification of physical and chemical properties of alumina are being drawn more tightly as the particular requirements of individual reduction cell systems are better understood.

The Hall-Héroult electrolytic process

The reduction process takes place in electrolytic cells in which direct current is passed through the cell from the anode assembly mounted above the cathode which is formed by the carbon lining of a rectangular steel box. This carbon-lined box contains the molten cryolite flux in which the alumina is dissolved and into which the anode carbon electrodes are suspended by current-carrying hanger bars. This is shown diagrammatically in the figure on p. 40 which is a simplified cross-sectional view of the multi-anode type of reduction cell.

Before considering the main types of cell, it is important to deal with the essentials of the process of electrolysis. The carbon lining of the cathode box or shell forms a cavity which contains molten cryolite when in operation. Cryolite is a mineral found originally in Greenland but now manufactured synthetically. It is sodium aluminium fluoride (Na_3AlF_6) and comprises about 90% of the electrolyte, the remaining 10% usually consisting of calcium fluoride, aluminium fluoride and other additives intended to control the physical properties of the electrolyte. The molten electrolyte is covered by a hard crust of solid electrolyte and alumina. At intervals, the crust is broken and stirred into the bath, whereafter more alumina is fed on top of the newly-formed crust. Thus the molten electrolyte contains a small percentage of alumina in solution which is decomposed by the electric current to release aluminium which sinks into the layer of molten aluminium lying on the cathode surface. Oxygen, the other element in alumina, reacts with the anode carbons to form carbon dioxide which bubbles off. Faraday's Law prescribes that 1000 amperes should produce 17·75 lb of aluminium a day but, in practice, just over 15 lb are actually produced. The ratio of actual to theoretical production gives rise to the closely-watched performance ratio known as current efficiency. The theoretical voltage required for decomposition of alumina is 1·7 but, owing to the resistance of the conductors, joints and electrolyte, actual voltage is usually between 4·0 and 5·0 volts. The optimization of cell design in electrochemical terms is concerned with the choice of current rating and density, anode and cathode size, conductor design and general configuration so as to achieve lowest power consumption consistent with cost and operating considerations, including the increasing importance attaching to fume collection.

Metal accumulates in a 130 KA cell at the rate of about 900 Kg per day. This is tapped off at daily intervals using a 16 000 lb capacity suction tapping crucible. The airtight lid of the 'cruc' carries an externally mounted suction-tapping spout which is lowered into the layer or pad of metal on the cell bottom and, as the interior of the crucible is evacuated by a compressed air operated ejector, some of the metal is siphoned out of the cell into the crucible. Meanwhile a number of unit operations must be carried out on each cell to keep it in a state of efficient production. These include crust breaking and alumina feeding as well as anode feeding or replacement, cryolite additions and alumina hopper recharging. Each cell deteriorates in use, partly by absorption of chemicals and partly by sheer wear and tear, until it needs to be replaced, which would not normally occur before it had been in operation for over 100 days or about three years. In order to maintain uniform output and optimize cell replacement, the latter sub-process is continually under way with several cells being disconnected and removed every week and a like number brought back into operation.

While cells can vary considerably in design, as can the layout of a reduction-cell building, there are two main types in use. Indeed, the difference lies in the anode design which, in the case of the Soderberg anode as used at Lochaber and Kinlochleven, takes the form of a single anode contained in a circumferential steel casing within which the carbon descends as it is consumed on combination with oxygen released from alumina in the electrolyte. The carbon so consumed is replaced by the addition of briquettes or ovoids to the open top of the anode on which they spread, soften and gradually bake out under the action of the heat generated by the process. Current-carrying conductor stubs are embedded in the Soderberg anode which provides a single flat-surfaced underside to the electrolyte. The other main type in general use is known as the pre-bake or multi-anode cell because it consists of an assembly of separate anodes individually supplied with current and in contact with the electrolyte. It is so called because the individual carbon anodes are baked before mounting on the superstructure of the reduction cell and they, of course, require to be replaced after most of the carbon has been consumed.

The choice of cell type is determined by economics and the significance in any particular situation of pre-determined raw material supplies and environmental considerations. For ten Soderberg design, the carbon plant need only produce carboh paste in briquette form. But the pre-bake cell uses carbon anodes that have been formed from carbon paste pressed into block form, baked and fitted with conductor rods. This results in a higher capital cost per tonne of pre-bake cell output. This, together with other factors, results in specific investment costs favouring the Soderberg cell up to about 100000 tonnes annual output capacity and marginally favouring the pre-bake cell with increasing capacity. However, specific production cost favours the pre-bake cell over the entire output range and, because of the continuing advantage to be derived from the economy-of-scale effect, the tendency has been increasingly in favour of the pre-bake design for new plants which tend to be larger in size.

Another important consideration is the suitability of the pre-baked cell for hooding in order to collect fluoride fumes emitted during cell operation so as to facilitate subsequent fume treatment before final emission to the atmosphere. Furthermore, the fume emitted from pre-bake cells is free from tar, a fact which simplifies and improves the level of efficiency attainable in the fume-treatment process.

However, at the time of writing, about one-third of world production capacity makes use of the Soderberg process. Thus the choice of cell design for Invergordon clearly lay in the pre-bake category but there remained various questions as to the optimum choice of size, layout and configuration, method alumina and carbon feeding, instrumentation, and a host of other options to be considered. This is a subject of considerable technical interest lying outside the scope of this book. Suffice it to say that the Invergordon reduction cell was based on a prototype design tested by Reynolds Metals Company on the development line at Lister-hill, Alabama, USA, in the mid-1960s and, as installed at Invergordon, was a 130 KA centre-worked pre-baked anoded reduction cell arranged in a side-by-side layout in four separate cell rooms.

4 Planning the Management of the Smelter

Early ideas and attitudes

From the earliest days it was recognized that the significance of the smelter's performance for the future of British Aluminium was such that effectiveness not always synonymous with efficiency, must be a consideration over-riding almost every other aspect. Really, the physical dimensions and characteristics of the operation had already been largely pre-determined from the days of the feasibility studies before public discussion and private negotiation began. Hence, although the capacity of the smelter and its location and much of the hardware admitted of little debate, nevertheless it became clear that, no matter how good the design and how careful the planning, eventually the most most significant determinant of final success of the project would be the effectiveness of the operating management itself. Whilst to many people this seemed a truism – indeed, the very epitome of the proverbial blinding glimpse of the obvious – nevertheless in fact it did represent a very important acknowledgement. It was almost an act of faith to recognize and state that success of a major project could and, according to this view, would depend on the ability of those concerned with its operation to deploy their resources to such effect that an adequate return on the capital invested would be obtained and that the other objectives would be achieved.

It was in this spitit that the so-called principle of non-comparability was agreed in early informal discussion. That is to say, it was agreed that where the performance of the new smelter was regarded to be at issue in any policy matter, operating management and those other echelons involved in policy-making were not merely free but were expected to disregard precedent and existing or previous practice in order to identify and define the ideal, the most desirable policy or method for use at Invergordon. This, in itself, was a very brave departure from convention, from patterns, policies, and even styles of management, sometimes carefully and deliberately fashioned having evolved over a long period of the organization's history. To allow or admit of such a radical re-evaluation was courageous indeed.

This principle was allowed to apply in the field of industrial relations policy, in the areas of organization design, and was evinced in many other degrees of freedom accorded to the operating management as it began to collect its wits and resources from early 1969. Even in those early months the first few members of the eventual operating management set themselves to work with a determination not to be bound by precedent and convention nor, on the other hand, merely to break new ground or depart for departure's sake. Mere novelty was certainly not thought to be of value. In many areas and in many respects existing practices and performance were carefully and closely examined as a basis for deliberate design of personnel and operating policies.

To be sure, much of this expressed itself in a rather school-boyish zeal as, for example, determination that no neighbouring organization, either in Britain or elsewhere, would be seen to start work earlier, to work harder or longer or with more objectivity than those involved in the smelter project. This was, quite understandably, regarded by those not so involved with a certain wry amusement, even to the extent of being described as the 'hair-shirt' philosophy. This comment was, perhaps, not wholly inappropriate inasmuch as many of the people involved in this fairly small group were working in seclusion, separated from wives and families, and with an almost monastic dedication. Perhaps the only real justification of the categorization would be to the effect that there was a degree of conscious self-awareness to be seen, sometimes mistaken for affectation. Newcomers joining the group usually regarded it as a mark of achievement or recognition to belong. It was made clear formally and informally that those given this privilege would be expected not to abuse it. In overseas visits the importance of being seen to behave in an enthusiastic, serious, organized, systematic and – I repeat – dedicated way was explicitly adopted, recognized and promoted. The group worked very hard indeed at earning a reputation, both because it believed that those involved should work in this way and because it was felt that a certain calculation was necessary to ensure that there were no slip-ups and no early blemishes to tarnish a reputation which, it was thought, might stand the whole organization in good stead at a later date when sympathetic understanding, cooperation and the assistance of many people and agencies without intimate knowledge of what was involved might be required.

The calculation came later, the enthusiasm and stimulus earlier; I believe the latter flowed and evolved into the former. I think, too, it is reasonable to suggest that here was the true beginning of the organizational style which was certainly oriented towards achievement rather than for affiliation. That is to say there was an early emphasis on accountability and personal responsibility; an avowed tolerance of risk innovation; it was hoped and intended that there would be recognition and reward for performance; there was a very strong belief in the place of the individual as part of a team and a tangible awareness of this factor; and all of these were intended to aspire and did aspire to high performance standards.

There was again an element of calculation in the belief that one of the advantages of developing on a green field site was the ability to eliminate from the beginning such so-called 'dissatisfiers' as existing historical, traditional problems to do with previous company policy and administration, salary structures, inter-personal relationships and working conditions associated with other locations and situations. If these 'dissatisfiers' could have been diminished (if not eliminated), and emphasis placed on the so-called 'motivators' aimed at bringing about attitudes appropriate to high performance, placing value on achievement, recognition, the intrinsic interest and satisfaction of the work itself, of responsibility, and the possibility of advancement, a priceless strength would have been acquired. All of these, it was felt, it should have been possible to introduce, enhance and exploit on a green field site.

Here we see the development of a clearly recognizable management style in the early days of the organization during 1969 and 1970. Those involved, reading widely in both technical and other literature at the time, were not surprised to find that there was much evidence, particularly in the fields of behavioural science, lending academic and theoretical support to the beliefs, attitudes and opinions which had emerged in the course of these early discussions. All of this tended to promote freedom of action of the executives joining early. It would probably not be exaggerating to say that this very degree of freedom, the ability to take part in

the design of their own jobs, to plan the organization of the department
ments either which they would control or within which they would
work, was a major asset in attracting some of the brightest, most
energetic and fertile minds in the company.

Organization structure design

No wonder the very structure of the organization came to be
affected by the thinking and developments outlined above. The
importance of unitary responsibility was recognized and intended
to mean every man having only one boss and knowing exactly his
boss, both by name and by job title. The importance of the span
of control of any superior was to be sufficiently small to enable
him to devote the time to the leadership and motivation of each
individual in his group whom he must know well in order to
evoke the necessary level of performance. It was of equal and
conflicting importance to ensure that the number of levels in the
hierarchy was not so great that there was a sense of separation
between the apex of the pyramid (as organizations are convention-
ally represented) and the base. After some discussion there was a
search for a broad, shallow pyramid design which did not at the
same time impart undue importance to the traditional organization
chart structure and design. On the contrary, importance was
attached to defining roles and, in particular, to delineating the
limitations placed on these roles – the constraints and parameters
beyond which an individual was not free to roam without reference
and without negotiating special licence or consent.

In adopting a rather conventional division for the operating
management organization structure, whereby the main grouping
was to be functional in the sense that all the engineers were to be
grouped under the engineering manager and so on, the reasoning
was not so much the traditional use of this structure as the belief
that this would aid role definition and would aid both individuals
and the organization in developing a common understanding as
to the purpose behind each position within the organization. An
interesting case in point is the role of the technical service department. The use of the word 'department' was taken to mean, when
a glossary of terms was adopted, a sub-division of a function
reflecting the principal groupings to which I have just referred.

The technical service function was regarded as the resource from which technological support, information, advice, analysis, fault-finding and trouble-shooting, could be sought on the part of those concerned with the actual operation of either process, i.e. production equipment, or the operation of engineering, i.e. maintenance equipment, men and materials. So there were to be two line-management functions (production and engineering) with a technical function in support to provide the so-called 'cab-rank' service . . . when you wanted a cab, you dialled the cab-rank – when you wanted advice, recommendation or decision outside your own terms of reference, you dialled the technical service department. This was deliberately intended to free production and engineering personnel for the prime problems and tasks of organizing men, leading them and evoking the performance standards in the utilization of machinery and materials. Simple to the point of crudity, no doubt, but easily understandable – that in itself being probably a real virtue in the early days of a young organization.

Similarly, the operating functions were expected to act in a line management capacity all the way down within the parameters defined as appropriate to each post. The accounting function and the personnel function were to operate in much the same way as the technical function, each with its own responsibilities and tasks and each of course including a line organization within its own boundaries. But the management of men where they congregated in the largest numbers in production and engineering was clearly and deliberately intended to remain in the hands of the successive ranks of superiors and subordinates. Coordination of uniform policy, the initiation of change, specialist advice – there were roles aplenty for the specialist.

Comparative experience

In planning the operating system, attention was paid to comparable systems already in being (some of which were of recent origin) within the aluminium industry in Britain, USA, Canada and Scandinavia. Searching studies were made of different approaches to comparable operating situations and these were informative. They had need to be because the industry is not well documented in published material, partly because of the secretive policies of several very large companies. However, the dangers of planning the future by relying on past history, and that confined to one industry, were evident. In addition to a deliberate attempt to think forward in conceptual terms, a search was made for information on comparable experience of green field site development of operating systems. This search was largely unrewarded but mention needs to be made of the account given by E. J. Miller and A. K. Rice in *Systems of Organisation* published by the Tavistock Press, of the relationship between the design and construction system and the organization-building system in the case of a new steelworks project. This account deals with the organization boundaries between the temporary task system set up to design and build the new works, while alongside and concurrently an organization building system is engaged in the transitional task of designing and creating an operating system. Nowhere else was it possible to discover such an objective and candid description of the interactions taking place between two such systems and the implications which these have for the successful accomplishment of the 'project'. Reference is made to the different perceptions of the final goal of the project held by participants in the two temporary and transitional systems.

There was recognition in BA of the need to obviate eventual operating difficulties and inefficiencies by ensuring that, so far as possible, the buildings and equipment would be designed so as to provide for optimum performance. Ostensibly this was the principal reason for the early creation of the operating nucleus. But, given the magnitude of the engineering project it is not surprising that, in retrospect, the transitional problems as between the construction and operating phases were seen largely in terms of hardware and technology. Much of what Miller writes in his 1962 paper could have been used to better effect in anticipating the problems which did occur at Invergordon (and also at Anglesey and Lynemouth). Yet, at the same time, much was anticipated and, indeed, the foreseeable problems were largely overcome. There were others which were not, perhaps, predictable.

Research work

With a view to obtaining an independent view of the problems involved in the task of organization design with particular reference to defining the role of the production supervisor, it was arranged for a study to be carried out by a research student at the Imperial College of Science and Technology (University of London). The report, by P. A. Gold, published in September 1969, was based on direct observations at two established smelters as well as a series of interviews with the managements of these smelters and the new smelter. It was concluded that the role of the supervisor changes with changing technology and, indeed, the relationship between technology and organization structure was the subject of the classic study of industry in south Essex described by Joan Woodward in her book *Management and Technology*.

The criterion of the appropriateness of an organisational structure must be the extent to which it furthers the objectives of the firm, not . . . the degree to which it conforms to a prescribed pattern. There can be no one best way of organising a business.

Thus Professor Woodward* goes on to remark that

leadership must be directive, participant or laissez-faire according to circumstances.

In describing the results of a study of 91 % of the firms in south Essex with over 100 employees, it was observed that large-batch and mass-production firms generally conformed to the traditional line-and-staff pattern whereas, in process-production firms, the line-and-staff pattern broke down in practice. Process firms tended to move towards functional organization of the kind advocated by F. W. Taylor (sometimes called the founder of scientific management and author of *Shop Management* published by Harper Bros, New York and London 1910) or to do without specialists and incorporate scientific and technical knowledge in the direct executive hierarchy. As a result, technical competence in line supervision was again important, although now the demand was for scientific knowledge rather than technical 'know-how'. It appeared from the study that some factors – the relaxation of pressure, the smaller working groups, the increasing ratio of supervisors to operators, and the reduced need for labour economy – were conducive to industrial peace in process production. The production system seemed more important in determining the quality of human relations than did the numbers employed.

* The late Miss Joan Woodward was Reader in Industrial Sociology at Imperial College at the time and later was appointed Professor of Industrial Psychology at the same university.

The observations paraphrased above relate to broad categories into which production was classified and it could not be said that relaxation of pressure or reduced need for labour economy were other than relative comparisons as between an aluminium smelter and motor industry assembly-line production.

It emerged from follow-up studies in the same research project that the number and nature of management decisions that had to be made also depended on the technical demands of the manufacturing process.

In process production:

(a) Policy decisions were fewer than in mass or unit production but committed the firms concerned further into the future. One firm was planning to erect a new plant which . . . would take three years to build and twenty years to give an adequate return on the investment. Production facilities, once determined, would be extremely inflexible, as in most other chemical plants. . . .

(b) Problem-solving decisions, on the other hand, had to be made as near as possible to the point at which the crisis occurred; they were normally associated with operational difficulties and were of great urgency. Policy decisions were even more distinct from problem-solving decisions than in mass production.

(c) Making decisions became an increasingly rational process. The imponderable became progressively fewer and the consequences of a particular course of action could be foreseen more exactly; management hunches were required less and less. This is probably the most important single factor linking technology with organisation and it has far-reaching-implications. . . .

Effects of increased rationality in process production. Discussions with managers and supervisors showed that this increased rationality in decision-making meant that:

(1) Any two individuals, having similar qualifications and background training and knowing the same set of facts, tended to make the same decisions, except on the relatively few occasions where value judgments were involved. This made it much easier to delegate responsibility for decision-making. In less technically advanced industry managers were often afraid that decisions made by their subordinates might embarrass them. They found delegation easier if they could be confident that over a wide area their subordinates would make much the same decisions as themselves.

(2) Decisions rarely got reversed at every stage up the hierarchy as they did in unit and mass production. The result was that in process

production far greater feelings of satisfaction and independence were associated with lower management responsibilities.

(3) Joint policy decisions at board level were more easily reached; moreover they tended to be those of which junior management approved and would have made themselves in similar circumstances. There was a marked trend towards the Executive Board, consisting of a high proportion of technically qualified directors, and management by committee appeared to work better. Another marked characteristic was the absence of an authoritarian personality at the top.

(4) Because responsibility for problem-solving decisions was extensively delegated, and responsibility for major policy decisions was retained at board level, the senior executive in process industry appeared to make far fewer decisions himself than his counterpart in unit or mass production. He therefore spent more time on his formal social duties as the head of a large organisation, which are so important to its corporate life. Also, the emphasis of his job was on the co-ordinating and controlling elements in the management process. He did, of course, make the relatively few decisions that depended almost entirely on value judgments, many of them in the field of human relations. This meant that, on the whole, decisions about people were taken at a higher level.

(5) Management performance became easier to measure as technology advanced. This, together with the need for technical competence in management staff, made selection for promotion much less subjective and reduced the strain and stress associated with promotion. The tendency for one individual to attach himself to another, and rise of fall with him, was much less marked.

(6) In general the behaviour of managers was conditioned more by their position in the organization than by their personalities. An extreme example of this was found in one large continuous-flow plant, where there had been 100 per cent turnover of managerial and supervisory staff above the rank of foreman in three and a half years. Some of the staff had been promoted from one job to another, but many had come in during that period from the company's other production units, from universities, or from outside firms. In spite of this the factory operated very successfully and it seemed that, in all vital respects, one plant manager behaved in very much the same way as his predecessor had done or as his successor was likely to do. . . .

At the top of the scale the exercise of control was so mechanical and exact that pressure on people was again at a minimum. Productivity was related only indirectly to human effort; on the whole, people were hard-pressed only when things went wrong. Moreover, the plant itself constituted a framework of discipline and control. Any demands on the operators were in fact made by the process rather than by supervision.

Most of those interviewed seemed to resent authority less when exercised over them by the process than by a superior.

As technology advances the entire concept of authority in industry may have to change. In process firms the relationship between superior and subordinate was much more like that between a travel agent and his clients than that between a foreman and operators in mass production. The process foreman's job was to arrange things within limits, set by the plant, which both he and the operators understood and accepted. This common understanding and appreciation of the demands of the job is much the same as that found in unit production.

There is, for example, a different attitude to time-keeping. In the mass-production firms visited, the foremen had to work hard to prevent their operators from slipping off to wash their hands or to gather at the clock before finishing time; but in the process firms operators would arrive early for the night-shift of their own free will in order to allow the men they were relieving to get away for a quick drink at the local before closing time. The process workers were aware that the plant could not be left unattended and they themselves made the necessary arrangements.

There appear to be considerable differences between production systems in the extent to which the 'situational demands' create conditions conducive to human happiness. Managers and supervisors get more satisfaction from their jobs at the advanced levels of technology; from the operator's point of view, too, it would appear that the relaxation of pressure and the higher quality of relationships between supervisor and subordinates will more than compensate for any increased monotony and boredom arising from monitoring occupations.

In conclusion, Professor Woodward summed up in writing that technical changes not associated with changes either in objectives or the production system would be unlikely to create very much disturbance in the organizational pattern. Where, however, the proposed technical change appeared to be likely to create new 'situational demands', these could be foreseen by a systematic analysis of the new technology.

Systematic analysis, both of the reduction process and associated sub-processes, were a feature of the basic and comparative studies carried out as part of planning the management of the smelter.

5 Development of Industrial Relations Policy

Initial considerations

It was apparent that the smelter could not be successful without efficient operation by a carefully planned and recruited complement of manpower. Obviously certain features stemming from the engineering design of equipment, site layout and materials-handling facilities imposed constraints on planning manpower requirements but, notwithstanding the importance of these influences, it was also early evident that the smelter would be unusually vulnerable to human aberrations. Not only must the process be operated quite literally continuously but the operating manpower must be capable of rising to meet the needs of foreseeable crises and also of dealing with the inevitable logistical fluctuations inseparable from lying at the end of a 3000-mile-long seaborne 'pipeline'. And, most important, optimization of process control and plant maintenance would only be likely to occur to the extent that the willing cooperation of employees was forthcoming. Management would have to be by consent.

Running through the many exchanges of information and opinion within the operating management team in 1969–70 was a growing concern that it would be possible to find an expression of industrial relations policy co-equal to the engineering dimensions of the project. Manpower planning in terms of optimum requirements for each task and operation, aggregating into shift and departmental strengths, was carefully carried through to the publication of successive editions of the manpower schedule. But these figures would be meaningless unless the underlying assumptions could be brought into practice. Here it was necessary to reckon with the realities of precedent within British Aluminium and, indeed, the rest of British industry.

Although the British Aluminium Company recognized trades unions at all its factories as a matter of policy, only tentative and even casual references to the new smelter had been made in the course of contacts with several trades unions at national and factory level as late as early 1970. Obviously management and several unions nursed expectations but no commitment had been made in the spring of 1970. Recruitment of operative employees was due to begin in June 1970 and could scarcely take place with out explicit instructions for the recruiting staff: it would obviously be essential for them to be in a position to be specific as to wages and conditions of employment to be offered to the responding job applicants. Once recruitment began, the ability to negotiate terms in exchange for recognition of any union would diminish and, in April 1970, the position was considered rather deliberately in the terms set out in the next four sections.

Trades union recognition or not

A   The initial issue is whether to recognize any trades union for the purpose of negotiating terms and conditions of employment and for other purposes, including settling grievances.

B   As none of the existing plant/union relationships within BA appears to be markedly superior to any other, given the importance of the local situation as it affects industrial relations and, furthermore, given the intention to establish the principle of 'non-comparability', it is arguable that no trades union or group of unions should be recognized.

C   The advantages of non-recognition may be listed as follows:
   (i)   Theoretically complete freedom to plan and establish optimum manning terms and conditions of employment.
   (ii)   All trades unions equally denied recognition; therefore repercussive effect possibly widespread but not inter-union.
   (iii) Freedom from 'sympathetic' strike action.

D   The disadvantages of non-recognition include:
   (i)   Relatively high wage levels and expensive conditions of employment arising in trying to defend vulnerability to trades union attack.
   (ii)   Certainty of unfavourable trades union reaction, perhaps not directly repercussive.
   (iii) Unavoidable need to set up domestic grievance procedure and other internal representational machinery.

(iv) Absence of external representation for conciliation purposes. Department of Employment and Productivity would almost certainly be unsympathetically inclined.

(v) Limitation on transferability of trades union members from other BA plants.

(vi) Inability to avoid recruitment of trades union members.

(vii) Probability of eventual trades union recognition under most unfavourable circumstances.

E On the other hand, recognition of a trades union or group of trades unions would have the following advantages:

(i) The ready availability of full-time officers of the trades unions and internal elected representatives of employees for negotiating purposes.

(ii) Narrower repercussive effects.

(iii) Possibility of creating stable industrial relations.

(iv) Possibility of negotiating favourable manning and related benefits.

F But the following disadvantages would arise:

(i) The need to negotiate any departure from traditional labour practices.

(ii) Theoretical loss or diminution of management prerogative.

(iii) Vulnerability to inter-union strife and unconstitutional action if trades union organization is ineffective.

(iv) Repercussive action by trades unions which have not been recognized.

G As the disadvantages of non-recognition outweigh the putative advantages and, as the prospective advantages of recognition outweigh the likely disadvantages, the balance of advantage appears to lie in favour of recognition.

Trades unions for recognition

A Proceeding on the assumption that some union or group of trades unions should be recognized, the first issue to be considered is that of whether recognition of a single trades union is likely to convey any benefits.

B   The advantages of recognizing a single trades union may be listed as follows:

   (i)   Management has to deal with a single body of representatives, thereby eliminating the possibility of trades union interaction.

   (ii) The existence of a single representative system creates an opportunity for a trades union to develop its local machinery, procedure, practices and personnel to meet the needs of a single, large group of members – presumably efficient trades unionism is conducive to stable industrial relations.

   (iii) The prospect of jointly developing effective grievance and disciplinary procedures among other things and of developing efficient manpower utilization is likely to be enhanced by the recognition of a single trades union.

C   The disadvantages of a single trades union may be summarized as follows:

   (i)   Concentration of representative power in the hands of a single organized group.

   (ii) Prospect of repercussive action during construction at Invergordon and elsewhere on the part of trades unions which have not been recognized.

D   Otherwise the need for employees to be represented and for management to create and operate an effective set of personnel procedures is the same irrespective of whether single or group trades union representation is adopted. It appears, therefore, that single trades union recognition is desirable.

Choice of trades union

A   However desirable single trades union representation may seem, it may not be feasible. This could arise either because of a trades union's inability to provide necessary skills from its membership or a failure to recruit such skills to its membership. In addition, a simple single trades union relationship might be vulnerable to attack if terms and conditions were seen to compare unfavourably with those obtainable elsewhere under a traditional multi-union situation.

B   If a single union representation is thought desirable but not feasible in the present situation, then an alternative would be a two-union situation – one union representing process employees and the other representing maintenance employees.

C   Several trades unions have expressed interest and it may well be that Invergordon could attract the attention of 'white-collar' unions. In these circumstances it will be realized that, if we afford recognition to any trades union which can show that it has members in our employment, some seven to eight trades unions might become involved in negotiations which would clearly be undesirable.

The decision on representation

If it is our aim and intention to simplify representation, action must be taken which is deliberately designed to restrict representation. Any such course will be selective and will inevitably involve the exclusion and therefore disappointment of some trades unions. In other words, if there are advantages to be gained in recognizing any particular trades union(s), they can only be achieved at the expense of possible repercussions. Either the prospect of unlimited trades union representation is accepted with all that that implies or the possibility of repercussions is accepted as the price of attempting to secure efficient labour utilization and stable industrial relations at Invergordon. It is believed that the management at Invergordon is intended to achieve the latter objectives. Therefore the problem facing the management is that of selecting the most favourable trades union representation and of according recognition in the most favourable terms with the minimum repercussive effects.

Wage structures

While the considerations as to the optimum or most desirable form of recognition were substantive in their own right, even if one accepted the views of the behavioural scientists to the effect that wages are only one of a number of hygiene factors which need to be satisfied before job satisfaction and productivity can jointly flourish, even so the levels of earnings and their basis are extremely important. Examination of wage structures in Reynolds Metals

Company in America plants showed that job evaluation was in existence everywhere with all hourly paid employees falling into one of a number of defined wage grades. The possibility of adopting salaried conditions of employment for all employees was considered and rejected on the grounds that the term was meaningless and that the total package of terms and conditions of employment was of transcendental importance. Additionally, such unified schemes of salary payment for all employees as were in force in 1968–69 were few and of recent origin, of which few bore comparison with the continuous shift-working pattern which would inevitably be associated with the smelter.

It was decided to draft a wage structure using a translation of the Reynolds Metals universal job evaluation system as a basis for negotiation with the trades unions. The alternative methods of payments were reviewed, remembering that direct incentive bonus schemes were in operation in most other BA plants, and it was decided to offer a single hourly rate for each job grade. Clearly this rate would have to be competitive in the market and acceptable to the trades unions, not only grade for grade but also in terms of differentials. Such a rate must take account of 'dirty money' or conditions payments applicable in similar jobs as well as basic rates and bonuses payable elsewhere; moreover, inasmuch as at least two kinds of shift working would be necessary, it had to be possible to apply shift and overtime premiums which would be economical, compatible and acceptable to all employees. The advantage of simplicity in using such a simple system was extremely attractive both in terms of comprehensibility and the ease of administration.

Easy administration would not only be economical but speedy; simplicity would reduce judgements by supervision as to the treatment of special cases and would be easier to explain both to wage computation staff and to wage earners in the event of subsequent query. Again, a reduction in the numbers of elements making up total gross pay earned could be expected to reduce the number and extent of complaints and hence eliminate one category of dissatisfaction. But such a wage structure was also of fundamental importance if the objective of truly flexible use of manpower was to be achieved. Flexibility could have an infinite variety of meanings but a few will suffice to illustrate the point.

In the case of a man assigned to deal with a variety of tasks in the course of operating a unit or train of process equipment, some tasks would be more or less attractive than others. In the absence of any financial incentive or disincentive, there was neither financial gain nor penalty to inhibit the man in his approach to the job. There was no financial motive to seek a change from task to task, and this served to promote the concept of an operator accepting responsibility for all aspects of his particular assignment, including planning, execution, checking and cleaning up. So much for flexibility within the role of each assigned job, but what if unforeseen additional tasks were to arise? What if another operator's role were to appear more attractive? Within each grade it was the intention to ensure that disparities in wage earnings would not hinder management nor deter the man from assigning manpower to the tasks needing attention. The way would be clear for universal or multi-skill training and development to provide cover for sickness and absence on holiday while building in variety and judgement-requiring activities. This would clear the way for motivation by appealing to the creative initiatives latent in every individual. Similarly, re-assignments from department to department and shift to shift, as well as from task to task would be facilitated and not restricted by such a wage structure.

The outcome of the negotiations

These arguments were very soberly debated within the company and, for the purpose of the decisions to be made, it was recognized that the objectives were the achievement of efficient labour utilization and stable industrial relations at Invergordon. The choice of the particular unions to be afforded recognition was determined by the strength of union organization in the Invergordon area, attitudes to comparability and the progress of negotiations at the other new smelters. Time was short because of the period required to complete manpower planning before opening negotiations and the approaching recruitment deadline. In the event, it was decided to proceed to negotiate recognition of the General and Municipal Workers' Union and the Electrical Trades Union. These negotiations were swiftly concluded by the end of May 1970 and, early in 1971 the Amalgamated Union of Engineering Workers was recognized as representing mechanical craftsmen. The negotiations themselves could well have been involved and difficult for all concerned, but the importance of avoiding such difficulty had been anticipated. The negotiations which took place dealt not only with the recognition of trades unions and the careful delineation of respective spheres of interest but also with an explicit statement of the terms and conditions of employment which were on offer. The national officers of the unions concerned were given, in advance, copies of a draft two-year agreement comprising wages, holiday entitlements, job grade lists, shift working hours and schedules, and also proposed grievance and disciplinary procedures. They were therefore to arrive at the negotiations with detailed knowledge not only of terms and conditions of employment but very much more besides. The actual negotiations themselves were concluded in good time for recruitment to begin and for each employee to be issued with his own printed copy of the joint agreement – the so-called 'Green Book' (see extracts quoted in following appendices, pages 65–9).

This agreement was intended to provide a text for industrial relations practice in the smelter but also to be indicative of the mood in which preparations for operation were to begin and, hopefully, of the spirit in which production would continue.

Appendix A

Extract from General Agreement on Terms and conditions of Employment for Hourly Paid Employees

Pay

Wages

1.1 The wages for grades of employee covered by this agreement have been determined by using a factor comparison method of job evaluation. The method is explained in appendix D and the rates are dealt with in detail in appendix A.

Payment of wages

1.2 (a) Wages of employees will be paid weekly in arrears by cheque. The employee will be issued a wage advice note at the end of each pay week detailing his earnings and deductions. The pay week will be from midnight Sunday to midnight Sunday.

(b) If an employee is absent, due to sickness, injury or detached duty he may request that his wage advice note be sent to him.

(c) Claims against error or for payment, or other benefits, may be made relating to any period up to, but not exceeding, 12 months before the date of the claim.

Deductions from wages

1.3 (a) From the gross entitlement the employee's National Insurance and Income Tax will be deducted together with such statutory deductions which are, from time to time, required by Government legislation.

(b) Certain payments resulting from membership of company contributory pension schemes, sports and social clubs and so on may, on written authority of the employee, be deducted from wages.

(c) The company may agree to administer certain other voluntary deductions from wages on the written consent of the employee. The company will not accept liability in such cases for the lapse or loss

C

of benefit from any organization in whose interest deductions are requested by an employee.

Payment for non-standard conditions

1.4 Call-out payments

An employee who has completed normal hours of work and left the premises will be paid a standard call-out payment. (See appendix F.) This payment will be made regardless of the time spent on the job and will be in addition to the hours worked at the appropriate overtime rate. Time on the job will be calculated from authorized clocking in and out to the nearest 15 minutes.

1.5 Payment for overtime, weekend work, etc.

While it is intended that overtime working will be minimized it is possible that in certain circumstances operational requirements may necessitate it. Overtime will be allocated by management and it is expected that all employees will undertake to work a reasonable amount of overtime as and when it is required of them to do so. All grades of employee covered by this agreement and regardless of the type of shift worked will be paid overtime at the rate set out in appendix F.

1.6 Payment for hours worked into following day/shift

When an employee is requested to work continuously into the next shift or day, for example when cover is required for an absentee, the extra hours worked will be paid for at the rate detailed in appendix F.

1.7 Payment for shift working

Payment for shift working is detailed in appendix F.

1.8 Relief working

(See Part III(3) 3.2 (f).)

1.9 Payment during probation

During the 'probation period' employees will be paid according to the scale set out in appendix A. Where a probationary employee is working shifts no reduction of the shift allowance will be made and the employee will be paid full allowance according to the shift system he is working.

Appendix B

Basic Hourly Wage Rates (excluding apprentices and youths)

WAGE GRADE	CATEGORY	FROM IMPLEMENTATION DATE OF AGREEMENT +1 YEAR				FROM IMPLEMENTATION DATE OF AGREEMENT +1 YEAR TO EXPIRY DATE OF AGREEMENT		BASIC HOURLY WAGE RATES DURING PROBATIONARY PERIODS
		Basic hourly wage rate			Wage per week of 40 hours	Basic hourly wage rate New pence	Wage per week of 40 hours (dec. £s)	
		s.	d.	New pence	£ s. d.			
5	Craft	14	–	70	28 – –	75	£30·00	For the first 13 weeks worked 6d. (2·5 new pence) per hour below wage grade
4	Operator	12	–	60	24 – –	65	£26·00	do.
3	Gen. work	11	–	55	22 – –	60	£24·00	do.
2	Gen. work	10	–	50	20 – –	55	£22·00	do.
1	Gen. work	9	–	45	18 – –	50	£20·00	do.

Jobs have been evaluated and wage rates determined for required standards of performance relative to full production.

Appendix C
Job Evaluation – Method

D 1 The job evaluation scheme employed by the Invergordon smelter of the British Aluminium Company is based on a factor comparison method. Details of the scheme are contained in a manual which is held in the company offices.

D 2 The scheme was chosen because of its proved application to methods of organization and working entirely similar to those at the Invergordon smelter.

D 3 Essentially the method depends on a concise statement of the significant elements of a job, assembled in job description form, and assessed against ten factors:

    (1)   Related knowledge
    (2)   Job knowledge and experience
    (3)   Manual skill
    (4)   Responsibility for preventing loss
    (5)   Responsibility for the performance of others
    (6)   Responsibility for the safety of others
    (7)   Mental demand
    (8)   Physical demand
    (9)   Surroundings
  (10)   Hazards

D 4 Each job is assessed against the factors in turn and, according to defined levels is awarded a number of points. The points are added for the 10 factors and give a total number of points per job. The range of total points has been divided at rational intervals to establish a number of salary grades shown in appendix D.

Appendix D

| GRADE | ENGINEERING | CARBON | | CASTING | REDUCTION | PERSONNEL TECHNICAL |
		PRODUCTION	SERVICES			
5 Craft	Electrician Millwright					
4 Operator	Rectifier Attendant	Green mill control operator Baking furnace op.		Casting m/ch op.	Cell room op. Chemical plant operator	
3 General Worker		*Relief carbon op. Green mill gen. equip. Baking furnace craneman Green mill press Green mill sampler	Cell replacement utilities equip. 'A'	*Relief casting op. caster Induction furnaceman Sawyer Craneman Weigher	*Relief cell room operator Cell room assistant	Cell Control-man
2 General Worker	General Serviceman	General serviceman Block cleaning m/ch	Utilities equip. 'B' Rodding room	Recoveryman Metal transfer-man Sawyer asst. Gen. serviceman		
1 General Worker						Changehouse Attendant Janitor

NOTE: (1) * Relief operators will be used principally for relieving in Grade 4 & 3. When relieving in Grade 4 they will be paid Grade 4 Rate.

(2) For details of each classification see Job Descriptions in manual .

6 Management Philosophy

The basis of effective management

Any factory may be regarded as consisting of hardware, software and manpower, to use contemporary jargon. To put it plainly, there are three constituent elements which comprise any large manufacturing undertaking. The first element consists of buildings which house machinery and equipment, along with other material objects such as fences, roads, stockyards, pipes, drains and, of course, those things or substances which are converted into saleable products during the course of manufacture.

Secondly, there are the policies, procedures and practices which state and define the methods of operating the machinery and equipment. There are also defined the rules and regulations which govern the safety and security of the enterprise. Then there are the records, reports and correspondence – all the media of human communication without which such an enterprise would not work.

Thirdly, there are the people and all the intangible human factors which bear on the use of the former element through the latter. These include habits and attitudes of behaviour; levels of skill and knowledge derived from learning. Out of the vast array of other human characteristics, individual and collective, should also be mentioned qualities such as enthusiasm, conscientiousness, dedication, empathy, discipline, tenacity, fear, determination, compassion and courage.

It is suggested that an investment of £39 million in physical assets and the care and attention usually devoted to the second element are all too often diminished by performance largely influenced by considerations such as those mentioned in the third category. More, it is argued that it is as important to consider emotional stimuli and reactions in setting up any human enterprise as it is to recognize the weight and significance of logical and rationally explicable influences.

Earlier reference was made to the over-riding necessity of bringing effective operating management into being but it was obvious that effective management would require the consent of all participants and preferably the cheers of the spectators in the audience. Design of organization structure, planning of manpower requirements and the careful evolution of industrial relations policy had all been developed with an acutely conscious realization that all these efforts would have to be acceptable to employees as yet unrecruited if the project was to be fulfilled. Indeed, acceptability would be a condition for consent.

Management style

First-hand study of employee relations policies and practices in Britain, Scandinavia and the USA provided evidence of a wide variety of differing approaches by companies and individual plant managements but, increasingly, the observation of man management in practice and lengthy study of published material, such as the Donovan Report (i.e. the Royal Commission on Trades Unions & Employers' Organizations 1967), proceedings of the Industrial Society, the Institute of Personnel Management and the American Management Association, led, as it seemed at the time, inexorably to the conclusion that deliberate adoption of a particular management style was essential.

Observation of widely disparate approaches to the differentiation of status and availability of perquisites was persuasive of the belief that any particular approach was virtually indivisible. Any departures from what was (however unjustifiably) regarded as the normal pattern of behaviour would become the focus of attention and, at worst, suspicion. So the allocation of privileges and facilities must be commensurate with obligations and the entire approach must consist of mutually compatible elements. For example, if status was to be defined as a matter of authority in decision making or as a rank in a hierarchical organization structure, then privileges or perquisites should relate exactly to the position of the individual in the structure. On the other hand, if decision making was to occur as a result of the creation of informed opinion leading to consensus, then both the nature of authority and its basis would suggest that privileges would be not merely irrelevant or obtrusive, but positively undesirable. Visits to established plants suggested that cooperation and productivity usually coincided with compatible 'styles' of management. Evidently these are circumstances in which an authoritarian style can be acceptable and widely productive. There are also situations in which paternalistic support by an autocratic employer derives from a clearly identifiable wish for such a style on the part of employees, dependents and neighbours. However, it was also evident that in a number of locations there was a developing appetite for information or involvement. This evidence touches on a subject which has been avidly discussed in sociological circles in recent years and the approach at Invergordon was adopted as that which was collectively natural and habitual to the operating management in its formative stage. In the absence of substantive evidence to the contrary and in the belief that as David Lilienthal wrote in his book *TVA – Democracy on the March* published in 1943 by Harper & Row: 'No longer do men look upon poverty as inevitable, or think that drudgery, disease, filth, famine, floods and physical exhaustion are visitations of the devil or punishment by a deity' a decision was made for Invergordon. Subjective in large measure, no doubt, but *faute de mieux* the preferred choice of those who willy-nilly would lead the enterprise at its birth.

In particular, this style would be characterized by 'parity of treatment' for all employees, an explicit approach to information dissemination, the elimination of grievances by prior achievement of consensus where possible, and a scrupulously fair appeals machinery for treatment of grievances – above all, an informal manner. By 'parity of treatment' was meant the uniform application of terms and conditions of employment and in particular the consistent use of the same principles to the effect that in the interests of safe and efficient operation of the smelter, every employee would receive the same care and regard for his personal hygiene, comfort and self-respect, irrespective of his authority or individual position. This rather prosy and pompous statement belied the spirit and insight behind the style. Out of respect for individuality each man was known by his first name, as is habitual in Scotland among people known to each other, and this included everyone on the payroll until sheer numbers made universal acquaintanceship impossible – personal and informal. Similarly the use of titles acquired in military service or as a result of academic achievement were excluded and without resentment on the part of their holders.

No communication was to be inhibited, filtered, obscured or delayed by the interposition of needless formality, but let the content of the message be as direct, explicit and even formal as need be. We return to the subject of what has since become known as harmonization in a later section of this chapter.

Training policy

Inasmuch as training can only be successful where all wish to learn, it was established from the beginning that the bedrock concept underlying not merely planning and training, but subsequent management of the smelter when the time came to start operations, would be the firm establishment of line management as the authoritative but acceptable vehicle of decisions and response. Superintendents were to gain knowledge and understanding by learning – so would managers, supervisors and operators. From jointly shared learning would emerge natural authority. Mutual confidence would breed in the ranks of some 600 men, most of whom were meeting for the first time. So the process of identifying objectives, planned study, analysis of observations and formulation of working practices was adopted as the formalized and quite rigorously applied method by which new recruits to middle management were able to acquire the necessary know-how in all relevant aspects of technology, administration and man management. Training and learning were seen as devices not only for the acquisition of factual knowledge and motor skills but also as the means for developing mutual understanding.

Consultation and consensus

In 1969, the nucleus of the operating management did not exceed twelve men and they were seldom all to be found in any one place on the same day. The group was based in London and often worked late, mulling over the day's preoccupations during protracted supper-table discussions. Travelling and eating together, people from different functions and departments came to hear of each other's hopes and anxieties, plans and doubts. This contiguity helped to reduce the disparities in interest and outlook that could easily have taken root and become deep-seated within the busy months of that year. However, regular and frequent management meetings were held to ensure that common interests were discussed and also to enlist the broadest possible range of inputs towards policy formulation as it progressed. This was important in relation to the engineering project design team and also later on in relation to activities on site, but it was of central importance in generating broad uniformity of attitude. Nowhere was this of greater significance than in matters affecting employee relations in which training and learning were all-pervasive.

The formal communications system

As time went on and the management team moved on to site in January 1970, and as the first hourly-paid employees were recruited, these ingrained habits persisted and became embodied in the formal communications system. This system embraced a weekly meeting of managers, functional and departmental staff meetings, and also monthly briefing meetings intended to cover all employees. At these meetings each man heard the latest news from his supervisor and could raise any question in return. As stipulated in the Green Book (Part I, section 6 and Part II), there was formed in 1970 a meeting of shop stewards and management taking place monthly to act as a general forum and entitled the Plant Committee.

Harmonization

If neither communication nor understanding was to be unnecessarily restricted, then in setting up a brand new organization from scratch on a green field site there was a great opportunity to eliminate impedimenta from the start. To begin with, let us think of hours of work. After due consideration, it was decided to adopt shift changes at 0800, 1600 and 2400 hours because these were believed to be at least as convenient for shift workers as any alternatives and to be advantageous for superintendents with twenty-four-hour responsibilities. As an extension of this, it was decided that day-working hours would be from 0800 to 1630 hours for all non-shift-working employees. This would have the advantage that all line management would arrive at the same time as, indeed, would office and laboratory staff, thereby ensuring contact at two shift changes and an exact match between one shift and day-working facilities.

Another feature considered and discussed with trades union officials and others was the adoption of payment of wages and salaries by cheque. It was widely believed that this would be unacceptable to employees and difficult to operate. Various contingency plans were prepared but none were needed. At employment clinics and in recruitment, it was made clear to prospective employees that this method would be used and the reasons for doing so were explained. It would avoid the handling of substantial sums of cash, it would promote the banking habit and perhaps encourage both saving and domestic budgeting. It was negotiated, explained and accepted from the beginning virtually without question.

One hotly debated issue was the use of a single entrance for all employees – scarcely a reckless piece of innovation but one fraught with implications and involving inescapable rubbing of shoulders, perhaps some tendency to unify or identify with the enterprise as a whole. The reasons for separate entrances seemed socially ill-conceived and to imply a disregard for hygiene and the well-being of all.

Only one canteen was designed, built and used for day-workers. There was no staff section nor a directors' dining room. Certainly parties of visitors engaged in private visits were entertained to buffet lunches in the management conference room but the chairman of BA stood in line at the service counter in the canteen when he visited the plant.

As a further example, all employees were required to wear hard-hats and other protective equipment according to uniform safety regulations. A colour code was used to identify the role of the wearer of the hard-hat but not to indicate rank or status.

In other words, the distinctions identifying management status were greatly reduced by comparison with those still customarily observed in British industry. While this did not occasion much comment at the time, all of these changes have remained.

One other word on harmonization. The use of first names was habitual among the original team. It would have been artificial and contrived to introduce titles, academic distinctions and the use of the word 'mister'. To raise artificial and unnecessary barriers to easy exchange of view at a time when there was much to do and when traditional inhibitions were being deliberately eschewed would have been absurd and very obviously so. Harmonization was adopted deliberately and rationally – it was neither a gimmick nor a whim. It was instinctive to those who took the decision and it was compatible with all else.

7 Manpower Planning

The development of a particular approach to manpower planning

In truth, operations began with the recruitment of staff for the operating management. This started in December 1968 with the appointment of the manager-designate. There quickly followed preliminary organizational activity in order to determine the form and extent of the nucleus which would plan the operation of the smelter and which would subsequently expand into the full operating management organization. This required careful consideration because of the diverse nature of the activities in which the nucleus would engage, because these activities would demand a range of skills and experience, and because some of the skills and experience were also in demand for the design and construction of the smelter itself. Nevertheless the individuals concerned were readily identifiable and, in most cases, had already made their particular choice. The assignment of staff to the engineer project team largely concerned qualified engineers, somewhat diluted by men with qualifications in industrial chemistry or the like. The operating nucleus required people with experience of plant operation who would not only be capable of the essential analytical and investigatory work, followed by the unusually abstract type of conceptual planning, but would be capable later of implementing these plans.

It may seem self-evident now but it seemed hard to enunciate and persuade all those concerned the reasons for certain personnel selections in terms of this rather unusual combination of abilities. In the outcome, as was expected, several of those engaged in the planning stage did not move on to implementation. This was because their work did not bring out any particular advantage in terms of continuity or understanding, or because they lost their appetite as the meal approached.

After the manager designate took over his empty room in January 1969, the first part-time appointment was that of industrial engineering manager. This was to facilitate immediate detailed and quantitative study of manpower and logistical requirements. By the end of 1969 when the operating management went into retreat at Chesters (the Management Training Centre of the University of Strathclyde) the operating nucleus numbered 10. They were:

Manager designate
Industrial engineering manager
Production manager
Personnel manager
Personnel assistant
Reduction superintendent
Carbon superintendent
Engineering assistant
Cell rebuild supervisor
Senior engineer

The retreat was intended as a kind of shakedown cruise because some of the group scarcely knew each other and, with all the travelling which the various study visits entailed, the group had never sat down to consider anything other than specific issues and had not developed any cohesion or sense of identity. The occasion was valuable in this way rather than as a working session.

Soon after the Chesters conference, the nucleus began to expand rapidly with the expectation that carbon plant operations would be under way by September 1970. In the event, that expectation was not fulfilled. Even so, several appointments were already overdue. In particular, only two engineering appointments had been made and these did not include that of the engineering manager. Yet craftsmen would be required to maintain equipment which would begin to be handed over in September 1970 and time would be needed for training of some kind. While it was obvious to everyone that, for the maintenance organization to be ready to receive this equipment, it would need tools and materials, power and compressed-air services and, of course, supervisory engineers. But there was an extraordinary reluctance to recognize the equally important need for information as recorded on drawings, specifications and maintenance manuals, all of which was almost exclusively in the possession of the construction engineers and whose concern for the fortunes of BA maintenance personnel was, at best, secondary. After all, the plant was new, wasn't it?

It is even stranger to remember after the event that it was at the time that the need for organized, systematic recruitment and training for production personnel was widely recognized and supported, while the even greater need for careful training for maintenance personnel tended to be regarded as a theoretical concept, virtually irrelevant in the context of a new plant whose engineering personnel would be recruited from qualified and experienced personnel. This was found to be a revealing commentary on the role of the engineer in industrial Britain with further implications as to the conventional approach to operating management. No doubt it was believed that preventive maintenance would be largely unpredictable, a mistaken belief, but comprehensible. In view of the delay in senior engineering appointments, the engineering function was uniquely unprepared to go to work. It may be supposed that, if engineers were not required until a few brief months before work began, there was little for the operating nucleus to do in 1969. Indeed, the preparatory work carried on in 1969 and 1970 enabled all departments to fulfil the principal objective assigned to the operating management, i.e. to design and create an organization capable of operating the entire plant to budgeted levels of output and performance. To achieve this objective, it became increasingly clear in early 1969 that the full range of tasks and performance standards would have to be defined in detail. Unless this could be done, the objective could not be clearly established and understood; unless understood, specific preparations could not be made. Exactly how many men of what kind organized in which particular way working to precisely what ends would be needed? Only general indications were to be found in the feasibility studies and documents drawn up in the course of negotiations with the Government. So it became, to repeat, increasingly clear that a precise specification would be needed for every task and unit operation which, in continuous operation, would build up into the total work load from which, by analysis, the manpower complement and individual skills could be identified. It could be seen with equally compelling clarity that this would be a formidable task requiring painstaking and exhaustive study, repeated comparison of observed data and re-examination before it was possible to state with confidence how many men and women would be required to do which jobs, how often and for how long, etc., etc. Hence the early hectic manpower study visit in February 1969 by the manager-designate and the industrial engineering manager.

From this and many subsequent visits to study organization, manpower utilization and working methods, the first manpower determination was prepared. This document was the forerunner of the seminal document called the Manpower Schedule, which ultimately ran to eight editions by 1971.

All this information was required for manpower planning as a basis for recruitment, accommodation and facility provision. However, for the purposes of personnel selection and training, this and similar information was needed to identify the skill and knowledge content of each job. With these data it was possible to prepare written programmes of training which specified the skill and/or knowledge which had to be learned and, hence, the training resources required. Further analysis enabled personnel specifications to be written for each job. The 'man spec' defined the physical characteristics required, together with the educational requirements, attitudes to shift working and handling of molten metal, previous experience and any other factor believed to be of importance in selecting systematically.

Job description

From a knowledge of the process in general, it was possible to design an organization for its operation. Thus it was obvious that the main divisions into which production activity would naturally fall would be carbon-electrode manufacture, reduction-cell operation and metal casting. So the production function was set up to consist of the carbon, reduction and casting departments and in the carbon department, following the sequence in which the carbon raw materials were treated. There was a further breakdown into green mill, bake and rodding room sections. Similarly, it was possible to set up jobs according to a crude natural breakdown of activities into groups of related tasks so as to form a 'job'. Clearly there were various alternative ways in which jobs could be put together from all the individual tasks which together embraced everything to be done in making whatever the end product of each process might be, e.g. a carbon anode block. Each of the main processes involves the use and control of a variety of tools, machines and equipment. Choice of task groupings to form a job was a very important selection to make in view of the implications for productivity, efficiency and employee relations, remembering that this kind of decision is almost irreversible. In the aggregate, these decisions make or break a new plant. The cost of the study and preparatory work involved in reaching the eventual choice was insignificant by comparison with the penalty for error. This work was valuable in gaining an insight into the future activities at a low level in the organization. A great deal of useful information was established on which it was possible to start drafting policy statements in every aspect of employee relations as well as in process control. The preparatory work took the form of drafting, editing, studying, checking and revising work schedules and job descriptions over and over again. From a study of the engineering flow sheet and general arrangement drawings, an outline draft would be prepared and then examined in the course of a visit to study the most closely comparable job or task to be found in a BA or Reynolds Metals plant. Then the process of checking, editing and refining would begin, sometimes leading to a radical re-grouping or re-structuring, whereafter the descriptive process necessarily would begin all over again. This laborious but absorbing task was extremely time-consuming but also highly informative as to how it would be in the outcome. The carbon department preparatory work was carried out and completed first so as to be ready for the start-up of that department in September 1970. But the most important job in terms of numbers employed and significance for process efficiency was that of cell-room operator. For these reasons, it is appropriate to consider the job description for the cell-room operator as it appeared in its final form (see Appendix to this chapter) and, as an example, typifying the form and content which emerged for production operators. The job description is set out under seven headings:

1 Job title
2 Supervisor
3 Plant controlled
4 Main function
5 Decisions and authority
6 Tasks
7 Performance standards

and is given brief treatment in simple language. However, it is important to realize that the titles under headings 1 and 2 are *not* descriptions but titles. These words and those above were assigned particular meanings and were used exclusively in the sense of those particular meanings in this and all other smelter contents. In this way not only was clarity assisted and definition reinforced by consistency in the interests of good communication, but this was held to be a way in which discipline could be established as a habit in matters of importance. To be careless in such matters as a job title – by calling a cell-room operator a pot-room worker or furnaceman, as if these terms self-evidently conveyed the same meaning, would have been to invite confusion in a new organization.

The list of items under 'plant controlled' is not literally and wholly comprehensive – that would have been undesirably restrictive – but it does cover all the essentials using the names that would be used in practice without encouraging jargon or slang.

The main function was intended to be clear and short. The next heading presented difficulty in advance of operating experience, but the list of tasks is the backbone of the job description. Here are set down a series of individual operations which the cell-room operator would regularly perform and in which he must be skilled and for which he must have relevant knowledge. To have written out this list is to define the job and to imply the characteristics required of the man doing it. It is also to begin to outline a training programme with its objectives and standards of performance.

Heading 7 was also bare, having been entered in the 'dry run' pre-start-up period, but would later be defined and revised from time to time.

Not, it may be thought, perhaps, such an impressive document to emerge from so much preparation, but not only did the document exist, its form and content were a matter of agreement between the staffs of the reduction department and personnel function.

Manpower specification

Once the job descriptions were approaching the final draft stage, copies were circulated to senior managers and to personnel staff for consideration and comment. With an eye to recruitment, training and eventual handling of a variety of issues, personnel staff were often able to improve the job descriptions in the course of preparation. When the job description was agreed to be in acceptable form, it was registered and copies circulated widely.

Then began the analysis of the job description and supporting information in order to establish as clearly as possible which qualities were desirable in order to do the job in question. In most cases these qualities fell into one of three categories: physical, intellectual and attitudinal. Physical characteristics predominated for most hourly-paid jobs and were often quite numerous. The essential characteristics required of a candidate for employment as a cell-room operator were:

Age 25 to 50 (21 acceptable, if married; absolute maximum 55)
Male
Normal physique
Good physical fitness
No respiratory trouble
No skin complaints
No back trouble
No stomach trouble
Good hearing
Good general vision (spectacles, if normally worn)
Normal red/green colour vision
Capable of sustained indoor industrial work
Not sensitive to heights

These physical characteristics had been derived in discussion with medical authorities in the light of industrial medical experience at BA and Reynolds Metals smelters and were intended for use in medical examination of candidates as part of the selection procedure being devised.

It was judged that a candidate for a cell-room operator should be literate and possessing both average intelligence and average mechanical comprehension. Again, these words were not being used loosely and were framed as a basis for the choice of specific personnel selection test procedure. Important and, indeed, essential attitudinal characteristics for this job were:

Stable job record
Preparedness to work shifts
Willingness to live within ten miles of smelter
Willingness to provide own transport to work
Team compatibility but ability to work alone
Ability to adjust to intermittent exposure to hot, noisy and
    dusty environment

Finally, it was specified that a desire for financial and occupational security was an important attitudinal characteristic to be sought in candidates for this job with a view to employing men who wished to settle down to a long period of steady employment in this job.

It was believed that, upon the acquisition of skill and knowledge during formal training, practice and experience in the job itself would lead to increasing understanding of the reduction cell process with consequential benefits to the employee and employer. It was deemed *preferable* that an applicant for employment as a cell-room operator would have previous experience of shift working, be accessible by telephone and already be a vehicle driver. It was to be *hoped* that he would have industrial experience and have undergone formal industrial training and experience of manual work. It was also decided that it would be *undesirable* for an applicant to have had more than three years' secondary education, to have any O-level qualifications or to have had supervisory experience. In other words, certain characteristics were essential, others were preferable and some were undesirable. Personnel staff were to use these characteristics in setting up the interview and screening procedures for personnel selection as well as criteria of acceptability in assessing evidence of the possession of these characteristics.

Man specifications were systematically derived for every job category, including salaried as well as hourly-paid categories. The next step led to the development of both recruitment and selection procedures. Separate analysis of a different kind is also described later when the development of the training process is described.

Manpower scheduling

Manpower planning for the smelter consisted of establishing the nature and the number of discrete jobs required to operate the smelter. In this chapter an account has been given of the method of preparing the definitive job description files. For a variety of purposes, it was important to establish the target numbers of personnel required for each job category. More, it was necessary to know when the jobs had to be filled so that recruitment and housing could proceed in concert. Furthermore, it was necessary to have a recruitment programme laid down in sufficient detail for use as a management-control instrument. These requirements were recognized early enough to enable planning of recruitment build-up to be coordinated with smelter and housing construction.

Most important of all, it was essential to establish the manning levels in the smelter at optimum values and to arrange this with deliberation rather than allow it to come about as a consequence of a series of unrelated decisions or events occurring during the formative years. It was to be expected that, once the abnormalities of the commissioning and start-up periods had been left behind, the manning levels in existence at the time when the long-term process of developing full productivity began would be difficult or, at least, expensive to change. Far better, to establish what the optimum levels should be for given work loads, productivity, skill, wastage and activity assumptions. Although there were many imponderables, all the more reason to study those things which it was possible to investigate and measure, then assign tolerance limits and apply contingency factors if necessary. With this in mind, extensive studies of manpower utilization began in February 1969. These embraced investigations at both BA smelters in Britain, together with even more thorough examination of manpower utilization at five Reynolds Metals smelters in the USA, plus information gleaned from various sources as to manning at other plants in the USA, Europe and Scandinavia.

The results were circulated within BA in April 1969 and progressively revised throughout the next two years but the original work retained its significance throughout. The basis of comparison between existing plants was the computation of tonnes/man ratios for all the plants studied after eliminating extra or anomalous activities, such as the silicon plant at Listerhill, Alabama, and computer personnel at Troutdale, Oregon. The nett 1968 cast metal output for Reynolds Metals smelters was taken as follows:

Listerhill, Ala.	164961 short tons	
Patterson, Ark.	64739	,, ,,
Jones Mills, Ark.	123945	,, ,,
Troutdale, Oreg.	101209	,, ,,
Longview, Wash.	198000	,, ,, (estimated)

The last plant on the above list was undergoing a major expansion in 1968–69 and the output figure used was a target representing fully developed capacity. All these plants are large-scale operations and most had been in production since the Second World War. By comparison, Invergordon was being designed to produce 100000 (long) tons. For manpower study purposes this was converted to 112000 (short) tons. Detailed comparisons were made as to:

Casthouse   Hourly-paid personnel at RMC, Longview
Pot rooms   RMC, Listerhill, development potline report
                 and engineering data
Potlining   RMC, Listerhill and Jones Mills
Maintenance   All RMC plants

while thorough studies were made of manning in all areas at all smelters mentioned above. Thus generalized comparisons for, say, casthouse manning in all the plants could be made and differences in ratio analysed for cause and effect. For example, in the case of maintenance personnel, the manpower was summarized as follows:

Job title	Soderberg smelters			Pre-bake smelters	
	A	B	C	D	E
Mechanical	109	140	75	71	78
Electrical	48	66	21	25	30
Building trades	6	12	10	18	19
Auxiliary labour	11	26	11	25	26
Totals	174	244	117	139	153

These totals gave rise to tonnes/man ratios ranging from 553 to 1138 and this could be explained in terms of the obvious differences in building trades manpower employed in the pre-bake plants in the re-bricking of their carbon-bake furnaces. Examination of the work load at each plant showed significant differences in organization, equipment and jurisdictional or demarcation restrictive practices but these were only evident once differences in usage or terminology had been recognized.

In the case of maintenance, the feasibility study estimate for Invergordon was originally 619 tonnes/man but, after the in-depth 1969 study by the operating management, the definitive estimate was altered to 973 tonnes/man. This change was made because it was believed (as a result of the detailed studies and with a considerable knowledge of the implications of engineering design then well under way) that

1 Invergordon would be new, i.e. equipped with modern, more reliable and efficient machinery;

2 Invergordon personnel would be carefully selected and trained;

3 the smelter would be 'debugged' in commissioning;

4 manning practices observed could be improved on a green field site even in Britain.

This was one of the few major alterations to the original estimates and, in any case, the total of the alterations added up to an overall reduction in planned manpower. In the outcome, this was also a major error (for reasons that will be discussed later in Chapter 13) if only because the implications of a high level of mechanization for maintenance manning should have been recognized.

An altogether different situation obtained in the casthouse because the Invergordon layout and equipment were to follow closely the excellent new installation at RMC, Longview. A study in depth covered the following unit operations:

Horizontal casting
Vertical casting
Ingot casting
Hot metal charging
Alloying, fluxing and skimming
Homogenizing
Dross removal
Block and billet sawing
Metal weighing and loading.

At Longview the ratio estimated for full output came to 1523 tonnes/man and, as a result of the study work, Invergordon planned to reach 1436 tonnes/man on a nominal cast-product-mix basis.

As a result of surveys and detailed studies, such as have been outlined above, a definitive Manpower Schedule was prepared. The third issue appeared in April 1970, extending to a thirteen-page document comprising:

SECTION 1 – Manpower Organization
  Summary by department
  Department organization charts:
    Management
    Accounting
    Engineering
    Industrial Engineering
    Personnel
    Production
    Production – carbon
                – casting
                – reduction
    Technical

SECTION 2 – Manpower Build-up
  Monthly summary by department
  Overall monthly manpower build-up:
    Existing – 30 April 1970
    May to July 1970
    July to Sept. 1970
    Sept. to Nov. 1970
    Dec. 1970 to Jan. 1971
    Feb. to May 1971
    June 1971 to later

  Department monthly manpower build-up:
    Management
    Accounting
    Engineering
    Industrial Engineering
    Personnel
    Production
    Production – carbon
                – casting
                – reduction
    Technical

Appendix

Job Description

1 JOB TITLE	Cell Room Operator
2 SUPERIOR	Cell Room Supervisor

3 PLANT CONTROLLED

16 Reduction Cells	Alumina
1 ECL Crane	Anode Assemblies
Fume Collection Hoods	Cryolite
Hand Tools	Aluminium Fluoride
Anode Baskets	Calcium Fluoride
Tapping Crucibles	Sodium Carbonate
Alumina Hoppers	Alloying Material
Control Panel	Molten Aluminium
50 Ton Crane	Anode Butts
Wooden Pokers	

4 MAIN FUNCTION To carry out various routine and non-routine operations so as to maintain the planned output and quality of aluminium.

5 DECISIONS AND AUTHORITY

5.1 Minor adjustments to cells to prevent excessive consumption of electricity

5.2 Rectification of those faults specified to be his responsibility.

6 TASKS

6.1 Crust Breaking

6.2 Alumina Feeding

6.3 Anode Block Changing with assistance from another operator

6.4 Assisting another operator at block changing

6.5 Cell Tapping with the assistance of a 50-ton-crane driver

6.6 Beam Raising

6.7 Reducing Anode Effects on his and other sections

6.8 Inspection and adjustment of cells

6.9 Flux and metal transfer with assistance of 50-ton-crane driver

6.10 Housekeeping

6.11 Emergency operations

6.12 Data Recording
6.13 Simple repairs and maintenance
6.14 To assist on instructions with Maintenance Personnel
6.15 Driving of 50-ton Heywood Crane

7 PERFORMANCE   7.1 Output
   STANDARDS   7.2 Quality
                    7.3 Safety

MAN SPECIFICATION   Cell Room Operator

ESSENTIAL

Age 25–50 (accept 21 if married – max. 55)
Male
Normal physique
No respiratory trouble
No skin complaints
No back trouble
No stomach trouble
Good hearing
Good general vision (spectacles if normally worn)
Normal red/green colour vision
Good physical fitness
Capable of sustained indoor industrial work
Not allergic to heights

Literate
Average intelligence
Average mechanical comprehension

Wants financial and occupational security

Stable job record
Prepared to work shifts
Live within 10 miles of plant
Provide own transport
Compatible in a team but able to work alone
Capable of adjusting to intermittent exposure to hot, noisy and dusty environment

---

PREFERABLE
   Previous shift experience
   On telephone
   Vehicle driver

Not more than 3 years' secondary education
No 'O' levels (If more than 3 years' secondary education,
look for stable employment)
Industrial experience
Physical work experience
No supervisory experience
Formal industrial training

---

8 Personnel Recruitment and Selection

Manpower planning had produced a set of personnel specifications and a schedule of the manpower build-up required for each department to be ready to take over when construction and commissioning reached completion. All the preparatory study and analysis had led to the production of an agreed plan. What was wanted was known and it now remained to implement said plan. Too often execution is regarded as the easy part of the management cycle of forecasting, planning, executing, coordinating and controlling and, if it is to repeat a truism, it is nevertheless worth reiterating the quintessential importance of efficient execution. The execution of the plan consists of three separate processes: personnel recruitment, selection and training. By recruitment was meant the process of securing a flow of applicants along with sufficient information to enable the personnel staff to choose candidates to undergo the selection procedure. The selection procedure consisted of a systematic and definite method of selecting those suitable for specific employment from among the candidates reaching that stage. Subsequent to actual employment, specific training was provided for each recruit appropriate to the job category occupied. The first two processes were designed and organized by personnel staff and the third was jointly sired by personnel and production engineering staff. The former is the subject of this chapter and the latter follows in the next.

In considering the recruitment process it is worth remembering the employment situation obtaining in Easter Ross in May 1970 just before that process began. Construction activity on the smelter was at its peak with over 2000 people at work on the Inverbreakie site. The operating management team was in occupation of the most westerly block of Swiftplan offices which housed all the TWW and BA personnel engaged in construction activity. On the fringe of the site, the Department of Employment was in residence in the old Inverbreakie farm cottages bordering the Invergordon–Newmore road. Inverbreakie farmhouse itself was being converted to serve as the BA (Smelter) Training Centre. Immediately west and south of the training centre stretched the temporary construction camp, housing over 300 men. There was no lack of work for local contractors and business for local firms. The district was busy and there was virtually no unemployment – scarcely the most propitious circumstance in which to begin a highly selective process of finding, attracting and matching the right applicants to the job vacancies. Here was the paradox: local support for industrial development had been drawn in part from those who wished to provide more employment and, when permanent employment vacancies began to appear, there was no unemployment. By spring 1970, unemployment had been absorbed in the jobs created by the construction firms. There seemed little recognition of the inescapable fact that these jobs were temporary and that the permanent jobs were associated with the operation of the smelter itself. In some minds there was no evident distinction being drawn between employment in a construction firm under the control of TWW and permanent employment with British Aluminium. A few held the confused and mistaken belief that employment in construction work either constituted employment by BA or a *de facto* entitlement thereto.

When the relatively small number of permanent hourly-paid jobs were advertised in June 1970, there were more than enough applications from discerning people to enable selection procedure to be undertaken in full as planned, successfully at that. However, as the build-up got under way and the number of vacancies being advertised increased, the number of applications per vacancy declined and the stream of applications remained relatively steady. There was, of course, a very large number of people who had written directly to BA, even before the project had been authorized, inquiring about job opportunities and proffering their services. In most cases, such applicants were advised to respond to specific advertisements for particular job opportunities as they appeared in due course. Contact had early been established with the Project Counterdrift scheme sponsored by the HIDB so that the most comprehensive coverage of possible applicants might be obtained. It was with this in mind, and the obvious importance of ensuring uniform treatment for all, that it was decided to channel all applications for employment in hourly-paid job categories through the Department of Employment. When a particular job was advertised by BA, those interested in making application for employment were requested to approach the Department of Employment through its Invergordon offices. This energetic and well-managed unit was now stretched to man two offices, including the temporary construction site extension, and had been kept very fully informed of the progress of manpower planning since 1968.

Indeed, the Department had also received many applications for permanent employment at the smelter and had encountered at first hand the simple belief that work on construction led automatically to indefinite employment 'at the smelter'. Perhaps the background of relatively high unemployment associated with intermittent periods of high demand for 'labour' at major construction works (such as the extended post-war programme of hydro-electric schemes, the Fort William pulp mill and, most recently, the United Kingdom Atomic Energy Authority Dounreay establishment) had obscured any ability to distinguish between temporary and permanent employment – a man was either in work or unemployed. With an eye to placing local men in permanent employment, the Department not only provided TWW and many sub-contractors with hundreds of locally-recruited construction workers but also took note of those expressing a wish to find secure, long-term employment at the smelter itself. The ability to make that distinction obviously implied a degree of forethought and even identification with the project which was certainly one of the important characteristics being sought by BA recruiting staff. As each job vacancy was advertised, the response was the subject of daily discussions. Every week there was a joint review meeting at Inverbreakie at which the status of all jobs was considered. Because of the definite nature of BA requirements for each job, not all applications received by the Department of Employment were transmitted to BA. To have done so would have been to raise applicants' hopes unjustifiably and to waste the time of D of E and BA staff who were already hard-pressed. Indeed, quite often applicants were not brought forward as candidates for a particular job because their qualifications were *too* high. What was required was a good match between the man specification and the individual's qualifications. It is a basic, almost elementary fact of personnel selection that to place a man of high intelligence in a job which does not require such ability is to commit an error, not just because rare talent is being wasted but because to do so is to invite frustration, boredom, lack of concentration, disinterest and, quite soon, inefficiency and danger, if not dissident or destructive behaviour. This error was avoided in so far as it was possible using careful selection practices but, where it was inadvertently committed, experience reinforced the view that to have recruited the very best people available (whatever that may have meant) would have been a thoroughly mistaken policy. Although it was deliberately avoided and, in the event, rarely occurred, BA was frequently congratulated later on having 'creamed off' the best men available.

The advertisements for each job vacancy were based on the relevant man specifications and these were in the possession of the Department of Employment. Once applicants had completed the application form 'Application for Registration for Employment – Reference ED1' the D of E compared the information supplied by applicants with that on the man specification and sent on the particulars of those likely to be suitable for interview to BA. The proportion submitted was fairly consistently one-third of applications received. The remainder were advised by the D of E of their future prospects for other jobs still to be advertised or otherwise processed in the usual way. Once received by BA, almost all those applicants were, in fact, invited for interview to the now resplendently re-decorated Inverbreakie farmhouse. This 'interview' was, in reality, a very carefully planned and controlled series of interview-and-test sessions, of which more later.

Reverting to the employment situation in mid-1970 as the recruitment programme began to gather momentum, it became increasingly obvious as autumn approached that, unless the response increased, it would not be possible to fill the number of vacancies which would exist in those categories requiring the highest number of men. In particular, fifty-six men (plus reliefs) were required as Grade IV cell-room operators to start work in January 1971. Cell-room start-up was still scheduled for 1 April 1971, with ten weeks' full-time training to be completed before then. Allowing two weeks for contingencies, 1 January was not too early. Before that, some men would have to give four weeks' notice, i.e. by 1 December. Thus the latest date for posting the last of some sixty formal written offers of employment would have been the Friday of the third week of November. Before then, some 150 applicants would have to be interviewed and screened for medical and previous employment histories; the maximum number of interviews a week was forty-eight. This was the maximum because the amount of administration involved in receiving a steady stream of application papers from the D of E and processing them simultaneously with carrying through twelve-hour interview days resulted in one week-day (normally a Friday) being kept clear for a weekly round-up of all outstanding correspondence.

If this seems extraordinarily complaisant, it has to be remembered that some 600 people were interviewed between September and December 1970. Week after week, there was relentless pressure on recruiting staff to receive application papers for about 150 men, circulate to appropriate departments, assist in selecting those for interviewing, return 100 to BA pending files or D of E, invite 50 for interview, while carrying through some 50 full-scale interviews in the same week. Thus 1800 application forms from the D of E resulted in about 750 invitations to interview and some 600 offers of employment. Obviously some weeks and some crops of applicants yielded more success than others and, when the numbers declared suitable for employment fell behind the Manpower schedule requirements, it was imperative to recover lost ground without sacrifice of standards or method. All this was to assume that everyone interviewed turned up on invitation and that all those offered employment actually accepted. More, it assumed that all interviews would have been completed early in November. With this in view, the prospect or drumming up several hundred applications for processing in the critical peak months of October to December 1970 seemed unpromising to say the least. What to do?

First of all, informal inquiries amongst those already recruited and others in the local community suggested that there was very limited general knowledge of either the availability of permanent jobs at the smelter or what the jobs might entail. The latter in particular seemed shrouded in mystery. In some minds there was an expectation of white-coated scientists fiddling with glassware in a laboratory, while in others there was a complete absence of any coherent understanding as to what the smelter employees might be asked to do. In retrospect, it was all too clear that the heavy emphasis in press and television on plant construction had neglected to explain or describe in any truly informative way what would be happening in the smelter on completion. In a district with little or no heavy industrial experience, it was not reasonable to expect that a community housing a variety of skills and experience variously employed in agriculture, garages, forestry and building construction firms would be able to foresee the kind of jobs to be found in a modern heavy metallurgical operation. They didn't, and no wonder. Not only that, how was anyone to know whether the terms and conditions of employment being offered in the recently appearing job vacancy advertisements added up to an attractive proposition?

The first attempt to explain the employment prospects at the smelter took the form of a public meeting in Invergordon Town Hall. It was not well attended, the atmosphere was chilly and the questions tended to suggest the existence of a self-fulfilling pessimism (later to become known elsewhere as the 'Highland Syndrome'). This was a most disheartening experience for the recruiting staff: some harsh self-criticism and re-thinking began at once. Once the possibility that there was widespread ignorance of what was on offer had been considered and taken to heart, it was a small step to a solution. In very short order, a large quantity of handbills was printed and spread liberally throughout Easter Ross in shops, hotels and pubs. These handbills invited men interested in obtaining rewarding permanent employment at the smelter to attend the nearest of a series of 'job clinics' to be held in prominent local hotels or halls within the next few days. A clinic consisted of a room manned by BA recruitment staff liberally supplied with hand-out explanatory leaflets describing each job and showing the terms and conditions of employment. In a few moments any casual passer-by could learn the details of the continuous shift-working system and the make-up of his guaranteed weekly earnings. Clinics were held in the nearby towns of Dingwall Alness and Tain, as well as elsewhere. Sometimes there were two on the same evening. Response was far greater than expected. The BA application forms which had been taken away so avidly soon began to return, duly filled in. In this way, completion of the autumn recruitment programme was virtually assured. A few clinics were held later in the year to fill up stocks of applications for the remainder of the jobs to be filled early in 1971.

Early in October 1970 full-scale employee selection sessions got under way at the Inverbreakie Training Centre. The centre was

D

equipped with a reception desk behind which sat the receptionist, who also acted as usher, telephonist, shorthand typist and personal assistant to all the recruiting staff. She was keen, energetic, good-looking and authoritative just as the personnel specification for that post stipulated. She was also the first personality to be met by each candidate as he arrived at the centre. After checking in against the list of expected arrivals, each candidate was ushered to the waiting room and given something to read. At nine o'clock sharp each session started and all candidates were involved all the time. The general pattern applied to virtually all jobs and consisted of a medical examination, a test session, a personal history interview, an industrial background interview and a 'personal chemistry' interivew. Each of these sessions lasted approximately thirty minutes and it was possible to handle eight candidates in a four-hour session in both the morning and afternoon of a day. As far as possible, the interviews were carried out in the same sequence so that the candidate would gain an understanding of the selection procedure and relax as he did so. As the interviews progressed, he learned more and more of the circumstances surrounding his job and its very nature. Not only that, the methodical pattern of the interview played down any idiosyncratic tendencies on the part of the selection staff who quickly became clinical in their approach.

Far from the system becoming stereotyped and lacking in humanity, a mood of objective empathy increasingly developed as the weeks wore on. Each man told his life story to the first interviewer who went over his application form with him and encouraged him to talk of his successes and failures, likes and dislikes, from childhood to his present job, if any. Then the applicant was able to ask his first questions before going on to talk to another interviewer about his previous experience in terms of skills, knowledge, aptitudes, preference and fears acquired in his working life to date. At this interview, the company policy to trades unionism and manpower utilization was explained and, again, he was encouraged to ask questions. Finally in the interview series came the meeting with the man who might be his boss. Other things being equal, the purpose of this interview was to establish the compatibility of the candidate with the human side of the job. Would he get on with his supervisor and his mates? How would he take to continuously rotating shift working patterns? Would he prefer solo to team working? And so on.

Meanwhile, a test session and a medical examination were under way for each candidate. At Inverbreakie a simple medical examination room had been set up, staffed by a fully-qualified nurse and a doctor. The examination was conventional but thorough, with concern for freedom from colour-vision abnormalities and histories of back injuries, amongst other things. In order to preserve confidentiality, the medical officer merely reported any candidate who did not meet the required medical standard as 'unsuitable' for the particular job, sometimes indicating clearance for non-manual work or another job. The test session took one of two forms. In the case of craftsmen applicants, there were written trade test papers, together with intelligence quotient; verbal facility tests were augmented by mechanical aptitude tests. Standards had been set for each test in order to establish test-result levels appropriate to each grade of job. Fears had been frequently voiced that there would be widespread and even bitter opposition to the use of such tests but, in the outcome, only two craftsmen refused to sit trade tests. In fact, the alacrity with which most applicants tackled these tests was impressive, as were the high levels of knowledge displayed by the craft applicants.

The interviewer entered the information gathered during the course of an interview on an individual form for each candidate, as did the test session supervisor after he had worked out the scores gained in each test. All this information was held by the interviewing staff as the day progressed until both morning and afternoon sessions had been completed. Expense allowances were paid by the receptionist to departing candidates and peace and quiet descended for an hour at six o'clock as the staff went home or down town for the evening meal. Shortly after seven, all those involved in the day's interviewing (except the medical officer and nurse) re-assembled in the large meeting room where they were joined by a functional manager, a departmental superintendent and perhaps another superintendent or supervisor from his department. Then began the all-important review session chaired by the senior recruiting officer with the functional manager acting as assessor or referee. The method was to take each candidate in turn and for the information collected from the interviews and application forms to be read out by each of the interviewing staff. The effect was almost always illuminating as the individual reports were heard in sequence, uninterrupted, until all had been delivered.

The SRO then began to draw out discrepancies and disparities, omissions and variations in the reports presented and these were discussed and evaluated. Often there emerged a general consensus as to suitability or otherwise. Only rarely was there indecision because of uncertainty.

The results of this collation of evidence were entered by the SRO (who had in his possession the results of the medical examination) on a selection summary form which ended with a decision recommendation. This decision formed the basis of careful checking with previous employers and other sources to verify the information given by applicants, special care being exercised when any unexplained gaps or incongruities appeared in an otherwise satisfactory record. Normally these checks turned out favourably. The candidate was then declared suitable for employment and the department concerned added a name to its roster of recruits. The final stage of recruitment consisted of issuing the formal offer of employment in good time for the recruit to give notice to his present employer, if any, move his family to a new house and be ready to report for training on the due date.

9 Training

Initial ideas

It was always evident that a very large training programme would be required to prepare operating personnel to run the smelter. This was seen to be inevitable however many people might transfer from other existing plants, either within BA or elsewhere. Not only was it unlikely that sufficient relevant ability and experience would be available, it was quite clear that even the most able and experienced BA men and women would be facing jobs that would in important respects differ considerably from their previous appointments; the totality of the challenge would face the entire complement collectively with a unique situation. The situation would be unique because of the magnitude of the collective task because of the risks of unforeseen problems whose impact on a new plant was equally unpredictable, because of the emotional excitements and pressures inseparable from such a nexus of so many paths crossing over each other after an individual change of direction and because of the need for compatibility of attitude and action if there was to be a reasonable prospect of success. And, of course, success was imperative. Surprisingly, it was indeed obvious to many knowledgeable and experienced advisers and consultants that a very large training programme would be required. But very few of those with whom the subject was discussed seemed to see beyond an admittedly sizeable schedule of individual tuition programmes so as to teach the trainees what was required.

After initial and largely administrative planning estimates of the size of the probable training programme had been prepared, it was clear that, if only to ensure consistency, compatibility would be unlikely unless deliberately sought. It was evident that training needs would include the acquisition of motor skills plus the understanding of simple process causes and effects and also common knowledge in all the many aspects of industrial relations and man management. This had become apparent to operating planners by April 1969 when a range of consultations was taking place. Yet even when (in the absence of any comparable anticipation or realization on the part of those experienced in industrial training) leading questions were posed to elucidate the ideas and knowledge which others must have gained, there was a disappointing lack of response. In two cases it was argued that, if BA would set down in detail the knowledge which was required to be taught, then both agencies concerned would be willing to quote for the job. So uniform were these blank, uncomprehending reactions to the invitations to discuss and, indeed, enlarge upon the whole spectrum of training needs and the various optional approaches that there was a serious re-examination of the basis of concern. The conviction was held that training must not only be thoroughly and effectively carried out, be comprehensive and uniform, but also that the entire training task must be an entity whose elements would relate intelligibly and compatibly one with the other. Something approaching a mood of frustration was setting in because of the apparent difficulties likely to face the operating management in attempting to carry out training solo. Then, towards the end of the inquiries and consultations, a meeting was held with representatives of the Industrial Training Service. It was evident that this organization had a clear understanding of the nature of the problem which had been perceived and, even more welcome, some explicit and positive views as to how 'training' should be tackled. Indeed, so thoroughly did the ITS understand the concern which had developed, so authoritative was the presentation of the approach to training and so refreshing and appealing was the evident appetite for the Invergordon 'green field' training consultancy assignment, that BA was faced with an easy choice!

The logic of the ITS approach to 'training' not only embraced answers to all the questions and problems which had begun to worry the BA planners, it also explained the interest ITS (uniquely among those consulted) displayed in tackling the assignment. Those other concerns, largely business enterprises in the training field, evidently were not motivated by anything other than the opportunity to obtain a business contract. The ITS position was also unusual in one other important respect. They were not willing to undertake the assignment unless the client understood and accepted the approach which they used. Most of the other firms had expressed willingness to carry out the training programme in any way which BA chose without seeing any possibility of ranking alternative policies, techniques or methodologies. Fortunately, ITS agreed to undertake the assignment after a careful presentation of their methods to a group of BA personnel and general management staff in May 1969. There then began to develop one of the most fruitful, constructive and effective relationships of the entire project. From the beginning, at every point of contact, there emanated the sheer joy and satisfaction that comes from working well together. ITS knowledge and understanding bred confidence and authority throughout its own ranks. This was contagious and, increasingly, the same could be said of the operating management. In fact, before the end of 1969, there was a strong feeling abroad that, whatever else might be in doubt, something good had already been found and established which would certainly grow and spread. It was to become a prop on which many were glad to lean, if only briefly to draw breath, and played a large part in creating the intellectual basis of the management philosophy and style that were adopted at Invergordon.

Training design

Raw material for the design of training lay available in the material prepared in the course of manpower planning. This material took the form of job descriptions, personnel specifications and schedules: it was capable of analysis in terms of skill content required. Requisite skills could be further broken down into statements of knowledge, practical operations and attitudinal content. But the design of training programmes depends upon a detailed knowledge of the skills, aptitudes and abilities which exist in the learner. The content and form of the personnel specifications were thus of great importance in designing training courses. In this we are merely underlining the obvious relationship between teaching or learning methods and the existing capabilities of the learners. Thus, for example, in order to improve comprehension which may be regarded as a component of knowledge, several alternative learning methods are available. These include the discovery method, private study and experimental demonstration. The trainees learn at a different pace and respond to methods differently according to whether they are school-leavers or 45-year-old men with extensive experience of life and work behind them. The learning methods to be used should also be chosen with the nature of training objectives in mind. It is, therefore, important to design a training programme which covers a variety of individual training plans so as to match the learning methods to the objectives appropriate to each job training plan, having established an accurate knowledge of the learners' abilities.

However, at Invergordon there was yet one central and overriding, quintessential consideration to be recognized in designing training – it was the view that training should be carried out down the line by line management. That is, each man, recruit or superintendent, would be trained by his superior – by his boss. The advantages of this insistence over the conventional use of an *ad hoc* training department staffed by specialist teachers are so manifold that it is extraordinary that it has not gained wider acceptance. To enumerate a few of these, one should begin with the benefits accruing from the preparation of lesson material (including aids) by the teachers, preceded as it must be by exhaustive analysis of skills and study of much information so easily and so often taken for granted. Not only is this a salutary experience and a learning experience for supervisors and management generally. In addition to improving knowledge and understanding of the industrial processes concerned, it also reveals the incompleteness of management's and supervisor's own knowledge and of the difficulties facing the trainees. Again, having assembled the necessary training material, no one faced with the task of conveying it to his own as yet untrained subordinates could very well fail to benefit from the necessary training in instruction given to the trainees. More, training in teaching is an excellent adjunct to and reinforcement of supervisory training itself. Furthermore, the reputation and authority acquired by a supervisor who has trained his own crew cannot easily be exaggerated, just as lack of reputation and authority often derive from a (sometimes) mistaken belief in the ignorance and lack of ability of the boss. Moreover, the adoption of this method carries with it so many built-in checks on the completeness and accuracy of the material, the capability of the trainees and the success of the training itself as to be so much more reliable, and evidently so, as almost to captivate the participants.

Preparation of material for training

Under the heading of 'knowledge' each department was faced with studying its processes, machines, instruments, tools and controls to the fullest extent attainable and with doing so by itself. ITS and BA personnel staff had the important task of prescribing methods, checking work being done and advising on the quality and quantity of progress. As an example of this job analysis as used in the case of process operative jobs, appendix A shows the four parallel routes leading ultimately to the production of a training specification. The diagram shows that each process operating department was required to work sequentially through the preparation of detailed and explicit descriptions of process flow, then plant, machines and tools followed by materials and services on to controls and instruments through to faults, quality and measurement succeeded by hazards and emergencies, reports and communications and finally work schedules. These were cross-referenced in writing procedures, methods and standards under the heading of 'practical operations' leading to a statement of requisite basic skills. All this work was drafted several times over successively. In several cases the full sequence was followed through by all the supervisors in the department so that all benefited from doing so, and also the material. Each draft was scrutinized and criticized by colleagues and superintendents as well as sample checked by ITS and BA personnel staff before revision, editing, re-writing and so on until, by consensus, a presentable version of all the information had been produced. This was faithfully tackled by every department for every job. The size of such a task should not be underestimated.

Job skills analysis

It is worth describing in some detail how these training programmes were developed and, indeed, going back to describe the generation process of a job description. This began with the writing of a brief notional description deriving from the provisional organization structure and the dimensional assessment of the total work load. This was the task allocated to each of the departments as nominally provided in the original manpower schedule. From such brief job description, usually written by the department head, there followed on individual analysis forms a mechanical description, a job breakdown, and a faults analysis.

Taking these in order, the mechanical description was a form designed to set up the requirement for the job in terms of knowledge of machines, tools, equipment, controls, instruments and materials – in other words, the hardware involved in the job. The job-breadown analysis form, on the other hand, was used to set down a description of the operating procedures, the methods and the standards of performance appropriate to the job. The faults-analysis form listed the knowledge of unprogrammed situations. In practice, the latter proved rather difficult to use but, having been tackled, it was in many ways the most fertile and valuable of the three analyses. Whereas both the mechanical description and job breakdown forms required careful and successive stages of drafting and refinement, the faults analysis proved exceptionally very difficult. This may have been due to the sub-title accorded it ('Knowledge of unprogrammed situations') because what might be regarded as a fault was, in many cases, not some invidious deviation from plan but merely the occurrence of some non-repetitive or unanticipated event which, in every other respect, was neither a fault nor any kind of defect and in no way attributable to a deficiency on the part of man or equipment. It can perhaps be imagined that the need to understand and interpret this concept proved extremely valuable in forcing supervisors and middle management to think deeply as to the areas and respects in which the performance of any job could become abnormal. This, of course, was not only more difficult but much more rewarding in its outcome.

Programming

Having completed analysis, using the forms and procedures described in the previous section, the next stage in preparation of training material involved the use of programming forms. These comprised the instruction plan, the plan for knowledge instruction, the plan for practical instruction and the plan for practical exercises. Thereafter a training timetable would be required, together with a record of training to be completed entered on the group training record. That is to say, there was a training record for the job category in question and also a weekly training record for each trainee.

At this stage all supervisors were trained in giving instructions (remembering that all superiors were to train their subordinates) in the methodology and techniques of training. This included preparation of training material, its delivery, exposition, the organization and control of practical exercises, the correction of faults, revision, and the investigation of knowledge and skills actually gained by trainees. After undergoing this training, using the material prepared before, each supervisor took part in drafting his plans for knowledge and practical instruction as well as the practical exercises. In several departments, particularly those involved in shift operation, several supervisors were engaged in drafting plans for the same job category simultaneously. This was useful in ensuring that the plans were comprehensive and took account of different points of view. Later these plans were put together and submitted to critical examination and discussion before final promulgation in preparation for use.

Standardization had been adopted for instructors' manuals. These comprised all the material required for anyone acting in the capacity of an instructor for a given job category. The material in each manual consisted of the relevant job description, instruction plan, plans for knowledge and practical instruction, plans for practical exercise, training timetable, group training and weekly training records. Manuals followed standardized indexing practice, including a guide to each manual. For example it was frequently necessary to differentiate between the operations, tasks and skills appropriate to a section within a department and the common training appropriate to all those working in a department. Again, this might break down further to individual job training within a section when each section of a department in question undertook differing tasks. Obviously much of the training for process operators was also applicable to maintenance craftsmen required to work in the same geographical area or department of the plant. This was particularly applicable to safety procedures and practices.

The final stage in preparation for training was the making up of training aids and equipment, together with a surprisingly small number of 'Do-It-Yourself' simulator units, particularly for use in training overhead crane operators. Hence the preparation of training material can be categorized as to, first of all, analysis, job description, and so on; secondly, lesson preparation; thirdly, programming for timetable syllabus, and so on; fourthly, resourcing, collection and preparation of aids and material; and finally, the implementation of the training itself, the execution of the task for which all the previous steps were wholly preparatory. Obviously, one other prerequisite of training implementation was familiarizing the instructors with operational equipment and materials, some of which were not available until a late stage in the preparation of the training programme. Equally, some of this familiarization was required as part of their own training and also as part of the plant commissioning and check-out work that was an essential part of bringing the equipment, as well as the manpower, to readiness. In acquainting themselves with the working characteristics of cranes, fork trucks and special appliances, the instructors were not only gaining valuable experience for use in training, information for use by maintenance and other personnel in correcting faults and defects, but were also, of course, gaining invaluable experience for use when the real thing came along.

Training in practice

As soon as the operating staff began to assemble, the activities in which they engaged were so planned as to ensure that training needs were being met on the job. Some executives attended external training courses during the run-up period; for example, the production manager went to the Administrative Staff College at Henley. But the great bulk of the training campaign began to move into action with the arrival of the first hourly-paid recruits in June 1970. These were the first intake of process workers (all of whom, as it happened, were named John). They were to form the nucleus of the crew that would start up and run the carbon green mill. There soon followed the first intake of maintenance craftsmen. Next came the bake-furnace process operators. Over the summer of 1970 these men worked through the successive phases of their training. On the very day on which they started work induction training began. Appendix B shows a typical induction timetable beginning with a welcoming introduction by the plant manager and moving gradually through talks, demonstrations and films in which the company, its organization and product range were described; all aimed at showing the new employee where Invergordon fitted into the picture. This was the beginning of common training, different versions of which were used for different jobs by the departments. These included the demonstration and issue of protective equipment and clothing as well as a site tour for each group conducted by its own supervisor. In the course of induction training the aim was to make the new entrant feel at home, familiarize him with his surroundings and acquaint him with basic information about the company and industry which he had joined. It also provided an opportunity for each work group to get to know each other and to begin to shake down into a team under its own supervisor.

Next came job training which comprised knowledge instruction, practical instruction and practical exercises. The syllabus for the cell-room operator job training programme began with a pre-training talk before going on to deal with cell-room layout, terminology and manning, then passed on through a total of ninety lessons on subjects such as instrument reading, 40-tonne crane, start-up and shut-down procedures, fume-hood positioning, basic driving of fork-lift trucks and reduction process. Each exercise had a serial number, title and purpose, duration time and target completion as well as explanatory notes as reminders for the instructors. Appendix C shows a sample plan for practical exercise for lessons 4.5BS22 to 4.5JS7. Appendix D shows the performance standards to be attained by the trainee on completion of the practical exercise 4.5BS22. These lesson plans and standards exemplify the balance which was struck in prescribing the lesson with sufficient detail to ensure that each supervisor instructing his own group would cover the same operations and to such a standard that interchangeability between crews and uniformity of understanding would be achieved. But each instructor had the freedom to exercise his own particular talents in the art of teaching and coaching.

Obviously the extent of training and the importance of proficiency and uniformity had been extended by the need to achieve flexibility. Just as maintenance craftsmen were to be multi-skilled within a broadly craft-based grouping, so process operators were to be capable of performing any task which had to be done by their group. The advantages of flexibility or adaptability in maximizing productivity and providing cover for sickness and absence are obvious. It was also hoped that, with such variety, job discretion and satisfaction would be enhanced. By this means it was intended to create circumstances in which motivation for high efficiency could and should arise. Remembering Herzberg's argument to the effect that wages and working conditions should be treated as 'hygiene factors' to eliminate dissatisfaction but that high wages and excellent working conditions did not, of themselves, lead to personal satisfaction for the employee (this could only arise from the fulfilment stemming from both individual and team achievement), so the jobs had been designed to include a variety of tasks demanding a variety of skills.

As each department took in its complement of entrants and occupied its own buildings with their own mess-rooms, offices and equipment, so the plant appeared to come to life. Nearly all training programmes were completed in full with time to spare. Some had far too much time to rehearse operations in artificial 'dry-run' conditions. Only a few were unable to carry out training to completion. This was only because of late equipment commissioning or sheer unavailability. Whatever else could have been improved had there been a second chance is not a comment which could realistically have been levelled at training once operations were in progress in earnest. The benefits and proficiency were there or all to see and measure.

Appendix A
Analysis of Process Operative Jobs

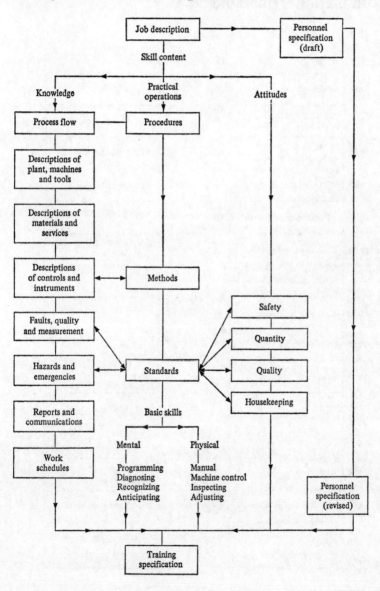

Appendix B
Induction Timetable

	GROUP A	ROOM	GROUP B	ROOM
8.00	Intro. to Mgr. etc.	(iv)	Intro. to Mgr. etc.	(iv)
8.30	A. Session with Supervisor + NI cards	(v) & (vi)	3IT.1. Course Intro.	(i)
9.00	B. Talk by G.G.D. or D.J. McKay	(ii)	3IT.2. Prod. of Aluminium	(i)
9.30	3IT.1. Course Intro.	(ii)	3IT.3. Ops at Invergordon	(i)
10.00	3IT.2. Prod. of Aluminium	(i)	A. Session with Supervisor + NI cards	(v) & (vi)
10.30	3IT.3. Ops at Invergordon	(i)	B. Talk by G.G.D. or D.J. McKay	(ii)
11.00	Coffee		Coffee	
11.30	3IT.6. Why Invergordon	(i)	3IT.4.	
12.00	3IT.9. Co. Policy	(i)	Site Tour	
12.30	LUNCH		LUNCH	
1.00	3IT.4.		3IT.5. Revision	(i)
1.30				
2.00	Site Tour		3IT.7. Terms and Con.	(ii)
2.30	3IT.5. Revision	(i)	3IT.8. Safety (portable screen reqd)	(ii)
3.00	3IT.7. Terms and Cond.	(i)	3IT.6. Why Invergordon	(ii)
3.30 / 4.00	3IT.8. Safety	(i)	3IT.9. Co. Policy	(ii)
4.30				

Appendix C
Plan for Practical Exercise

Exercise No.	Title/Purpose	Ref.	Duration/ Attempts	Target	Equipment, Materials, & Location

4.5 BS 22	*Hoist, Lower, Travel, 50 ton crane*
	Travel ten cell lengths, lowering hook from fully raised position to pre-set target height, stopping crane in correct position at that height for example, Height of hopper
	  „ „ beam
	  „ „ checkplate.
	Repeat in each direction.
			20 Mins. per Man
			
			5 Attempts
				80%	50 ton crane

4.5 JS 2	*Replace Anode Baskets* Using tractor and train of 4 anode trailers, load and unload the 8 baskets into position on trailer and along cell room. Assistance on floor.		30 Mins. per Man 1 Attempt	90%	Tractor Trailer Train Anode baskets 50 Ton Crane
4.5 JS 4	*10 Ton Bucket Handling* Hook bucket from trailer on to crane at working aisle. Lift clear of risers. Lower bucket between cells. Simulate movements used when banking up 2 cells (both sides). Cells to be 4 cells apart. Replace bucket on trailer in working aisle.		30 Mins. per Man 5 Attempts	100%	10 ton bucket 50 ton crane Trailer
4.5 JS 7	*Crucible Insertion Simulated Cell* Work from either side of mock-up. Approach with cruce in high position, lowering while approaching into every height. After cruce is turned practice entering and withdrawing pipe into and out of hole without touching sides. Assistance and check at floor level.		30 Mins. per Man 10 Attempts	90%	50 ton crane Cells

Appendix D

50 Ton Heywood Crane Exercises Performance Standards

EXERCISE NO: BS.22
EXERCISE TITLE: Hoist/Lower and Travel.

Correct Performance:

1   Movements to be made simultaneously.
2   Both controls to be moved in direction of movement only.
3   (a) Hoist control top notch to be engaged immediately for lower.
    (b) Hoist control to be moved up notch by notch for hoist.
4   Hook swing to be less than $\pm 9''$.
5   Hoist control to be cut back notch by notch as target is approached.
6   Long travel neutral to be selected several feet before target point.
7   Long travel coast to target point under brake control.
8   Hoist neutral to be engaged only after at least last $3''$ in bottom notch.
9   Hook to be at correct height within $\pm 3''$ of target.
10   Long travel to stop on target with less than $\pm 3''$ error.
11   Long travel swing no greater than $\pm 6''$.

10 Plant Commissioning

Organization for design

In the twenty-one months or so that elapsed between the author-
ization of the smelter project and the virtual completion of the
plant at Invergordon, a great deal had to be done. Whilst the
main subject of interest, as far as this book is concerned, lies in
the design, and the creation of the operating management, it is
necessary to give some indication of the work proceeding at the
same time during the years 1969 to 1971 in the design, construction and erection of the smelter.

In the autumn of 1968, as has been mentioned before, a package
deal management contract was awarded to the Taywood Wrightson consortium for the job of designing and building the smelter.
For this purpose, almost 200 men assembled at the consortium
headquarters in Southall, adjoining the Taylor Woodrow office
buildings. Here the BA project engineers gathered during September and October 1968 and formed, in themselves, a project team
headed by Gordon E. White as project manager, with R. C. Barker
as chief project engineer. Both of these men worked under the
experienced direction of D. J. Hedgecock, director of engineering
of The British Aluminium Company. His appointment in September 1968 emphasized the importance attaching to the successful
completion of all the engineering work which was about to be
undertaken and which, by virtue of his vast experience, Jake
Hedgecock was uniquely equipped to handle. A tall, lean, terse
Nebraskan, Jake had spent most of his long career in the aluminium industry, beginning with the Aluminum Company of America
and joining Reynolds in the post-war years. Gordon White and
Dick Barker were also seconded by Reynolds Metals Company to
work for BA in the design of the smelter. Gordon White was an
experienced operating man who had worked for Reynolds at the
Troutdale and Listerhill plants, while Dick Barker had recently
been project engineer at an extension to the large Longview smelter in the state of Washington, USA.

These senior men were joined by other experienced project engineers from both BA and Reynolds Metals: this team was responsible for defining the specifications to which the very much larger Taywood Wrightson organization would work. These specifications would cover not merely outline processes and the settling down with increasing detail of the parameters within which the process and unit operation must act, but also, where appropriate, sketch plans, flow diagrams and other material by way of amplification. The TWW organization had its own board of directors, its own project manager and its own group of senior project engineers, each of whom had an opposite number in the BA team. Under each senior project engineer, TWW had in varying numbers groups of project engineers, each of whom, in turn, had a senior draughtsman and a number of other draughtsmen, tracers, typists, filing clerks, and so on to assist him. At first, the two organizations working closely together were somewhat stratified inasmuch as the BA and TWW men and women working on the design of the carbon plant were much more closely involved together than they were with their colleagues working on, let us say, the casting shop.

Progressively these two organizations sketched, specified, proposed, drafted and re-drafted layouts, general arrangement and, finally, construction drawings for buildings, machinery and equipment. Along with the drawings, of course, went detailed schedules of materials, fittings, schedules of quantity and other lists which began to build up into the input material for use by the very substantial purchasing and procurement department which TWW was beginning to build up in 1970. After the completion of arrangement drawings, each building and area of the plant was developed in terms of the electrical process building services, including compressed air, drainage, water and other facilities. At each of these successive stages the proposals were issued for comment not only to the BA design team but also to the TWW representatives on site, to which was added, as construction of buildings began to arise at Inverbreakie Farm, an increasingly large BA construction representation. Here again, the operating management kept in touch, though not too closely, being aware of and being required to satisfy as to the process specifications both in terms of capability and performance requirements and of the facilities being installed. As the design work was completed, so was the definitive estimate of cost – a subject, as can be imagined, of close, hard-fought argument and debate.

Progressively following on as the designs matured, the procurement activities proceeded whereby a complete specification of the total requirements for each contract to be let was issued in draft and ultimately in final form for tender. On receipt of tenders, very thorough bid analysis comparisons were carried through and scheduled. These comparisons were circulated for comment, sometimes modified bids or tenders were called for but, before an order was finally placed on a basis of competitive tender, final comment was invited from the construction and operating management. If none of this is novel or in any way revolutionary, nevertheless it was carried out with a thoroughness and determination which was unusual and, again, if not sophisticated critical path techniques or computer programming and planning was adopted, nevertheless very close control was a feature of the design and planning of every building and every process train. With the issue of orders and the approval of arrangement, service and construction drawings, design material increasingly passed to the site for construction, installation and commissioning to proceed.

Construction

Beginning with the first movement of earth at Inverbreakie on 9 December 1968, construction proceeded throughout winter characterized by mud and rain. Indeed, the entrance road and a considerable amount of other early construction work were driven ahead with characteristic resource by Klaus Van der Lee, site project manager, and Ken Williams, the energetic Taylor Woodrow Construction civil manager. Over 1·5 million cubic yards of earth were moved, followed by the placing of 173000 cubic yards of concrete – crude, simple figures which give some indication of the dimensions of the civil-engineering work which preceded the erection and installation of mechanical and electrical equipment. Even before that could begin, it was necessary not only to build and equip construction offices which were very substantial offices in their own right but, also, it was necessary to build, equip and manage a residential construction camp with its own barber's shop, post office, bar, canteen – all facilities sufficient to house up to 400 men at full capacity. This construction camp was well built, well heated and competently managed. As a result, not only was the construction force adequately served but a facility was provided by the TWW organization for the use of all the host of smaller sub-contractors, each of whom would otherwise have been competing for scarce accommodation of a temporary nature in the Invergordon area.

Late in the spring of 1969, foundations began to rise out of the ground and the first steel to appear. To those who were to operate the plant this was exciting and carried a reality which somehow or other the movement of earth and the placing of concrete failed quite to achieve. The sight of those tall columns and the roof structures beginning to form seemed to tell something of the future and had a very familiar, indeed, intimate, entirely recognizable look about it. So the project proceeded through 1970 and into 1971 with the vast burden of the civil work undertaken by the energetic Taylor Woodrow Construction partner of the consortium. Let it be said that the surface finish of the cell-room concrete floors achieved a standard not hitherto equalled at any other smelter known to the operating management. As the buildings took shape, they were clad largely with aluminium sheeting. Another interesting statistic tells that 830 tonnes of aluminium sheeting were used in the building of the smelter. The buildings, once clad, were ready for equipment, the fitting of services, provision of power, lighting, compressed air, drainage, and so on. All this was necessary before the installation and erection of permanent process equipment, or even mechanical and electrical service installations, could proceed. Extensive temporary electrical supplies had to be laid so that site welding could proceed uninterrupted at the appropriate time in the construction timetable. The construction timetable, subsequent to frequent revision, was a principal item in the progress meetings held both by Taywood Wrightson, British Aluminium and also by the BA–TWW design organization at Southall. Actual progress was compared with plan. The differences were measured and, where possible, corrective action was taken. All the plans were modified so that design and construction was managed. By the summer of 1970 the carbon plant, consisting of the green mill, bake furnace and rodding room sections, was nearing completion. This was one area which did, in fact, fall behind. The commissioning of this part of the smelter was one of the most hectic experiences for all those concerned.

Commissioning of plant and equipment

It should be explained that, within the TWW organization, once the mechanical and electrical engineering departments had respectively completed the erection and installation of machinery and ancillary equipment in each building or open area, the responsibility of commissioning the equipment was formally assigned to the plant commissioning department (PCD) headed by Alan P. Muir. To this department was given the responsibility of carrying out an independent inspection of the machinery and equipment as built. That is to say, carrying out physical measurements, checks and comparisons against drawings, schedules, specifications and diagrams issued to construction by the design organization. Having satisfied themselves that the appropriate machinery had been properly erected, it was for this department to set it in motion in the unloaded condition, to check its behaviour and to make sure that it did, in fact, perform as intended. That is to say, where there was an electric motor drive working through Vee belts or a hydraulic clutch so as to turn a fan or a crusher, the drive would be checked for alignment and for direction of rotation as well as for the presence of any defect, such as vibration, misalignment or any other fault against a defined standard as set out in the construction specifications. A formal procedure was agreed between BA construction and the process-control department on site for the inspection, testing and rectification of faults of all equipment in all parts of the smelter. Very often, the list of defects found by PCD on inspection involved a great deal of rectification work. Sometimes this involved handing the machinery in question back to the mechanical engineering department for extensive dismantling and re-assembly in order to attain the required standard as set down in the construction specification. On other occasions, where the rectification work was of a minor nature, it was carried out by PCD commissioning engineers themselves, sometimes with the assistance of contractors. In all of this, of course, BA construction department took a close and active interest without relieving TWW of its comprehensive responsibility for completing the entire installation of the smelter so as to perform its intended duty.

As in most major projects, serious difficulties were encountered with uncompleted work or incorrectly completed work, delays in the finishing of ancillary services after the principal units had been installed that were serviceable in any areas. Sometimes, indeed all too often, adequate operating instructions and relevant wiring diagrams were not supplied by manufacturers. This made it extremely difficult for the last-minute design work, involving the putting together of coordinated schematic electrical or pneumatic or hydraulic or a combination of all three elements in a single control system, to be put together for use by initially TWW construction, subsequently TWW, PCD and, of course, ultimately, the poor old customer.

Process commissioning

The words 'process commissioning' were intended to mean the commissioning of the equipment in carrying out the process for which it had been designed and installed. This almost always involved passing materials through a crusher or a conveyor into a hopper at a given rate and to a given extent. In so doing, dust might be emitted, heat conveyed, friction generated, and a whole series of problems created which had not arisen during the dry-run unloaded plant-commissioning trials. The first process commissioning began in the late autumn of 1970 in the carbon plant and proceeded uninterrupted for the next nine months. This was an exceedingly intensive experience for all who were involved and long hours were worked for many weeks. By the end of 1970, the first carbon block had been produced from the electrode presses in the green mill. In 1971 there arrived in the Cromarty Firth the S.S. *Richard*, carrying 35000 tonnes of alumina from Jamaica. The ship was on time. The conveyor, with all its associated control gear, was also ready, but only just. It took nine long, weary days to unload those 35000 tonnes but, nevertheless, the unloading operation was completed successfully and without serious mishap – nine days by comparison with a specified seventy-two hours.

The question as to the extent to which process commissioning could be carried through to completion without moving through to a *de facto* operating position is of real technical interest for this and other industries. But clearly process commissioning had to be carried through to the point at which it was justifiable to proceed with full-scale operations. Realistically, neither in fact nor in theory, could process commissioning be carried through to a point at which the operating management could be fully satisfied.

Once process commissioning had been completed to the satisfaction of the plant commissioning department of TWW, their certification of this fact was passed to BA construction department on site for approval. Approval by the construction department of the BA project team carried with it not only full acceptance but also, obviously, certification for payment, save only for those retention payments that are normally withheld in the course of any purchase order where satisfactory completion is deemed to depend on performance in practice of the equipment supplied over a period of time.

Obviously the acceptability of this concept to the operating management was a matter of debate, but clearly it could hardly have been arranged otherwise. Responsibility for the design, erection and commissioning had necessarily to be vested in one area. This authority was given to the engineering project-management organization. There is no doubt that they intended to do their job as faithfully as could be achieved. On the other hand, the objective of the operating management team, whilst no doubt theoretically compatible with that of the engineering project team, carried with it the sting in the tail of having to achieve design-performance criteria, that is, the performance criteria built into the original economic feasibility study and on which the profitability of the investment had been based. This conflict of interests was real and was not based on any mere semantic set of distinctions devised for the vindication of petty jealousies or self-interest of those with narrow responsibilities. On the contrary, it was the perfectly understandable concern of those responsible for achieving performance using facilities provided by those whose responsibility ended when the facilities were handed over. Nevertheless, there were many benefits to be gained by operating personnel taking part in process commissioning activities. Obviously, this was familiarization with the real thing and not with a drawing or a set of written instructions, schedules of plans. This was an opportunity to get to know the particular characteristics or foibles of control equipment and machinery itself. It applied not only at supervisory and operator level but also, in particular, for the engineering-maintenance personnel, much of whose training had clearly and inevitably taken place in the somewhat unreal atmosphere of a dry-run situation.

For the very practical and thoroughly important reason that the start-up date for the cell room had been set as April 1971 and was approaching fast, the operating management undertook to carry out and complete the commissioning of several parts of the carbon plant in order to release TWW commissioning personnel for activities in the rodding room, cell rooms, casthouse and else-where. As a result, the first anode block crushed in the rodding room butt crusher met its fate seven days before the circuit break-ers in the switchyard at the north of the smelter were closed to receive electrical power for the first time from the national grid under the contract negotiated in 1969 with NOSHEB. This was too close for comfort. At the same time, successive delays in order that every last 'i' be dotted and 't' be crossed, every last joint checked and tested and every last instrument calibrated, could no doubt have proceeded for several months and it was about time that some practical experience was gained, not to mention getting to work in order to produce some aluminium and sell it in the market.

11 The Initial Operating Phase

Bake start-up

The very first set of process plant to be started up was that of the bake furnace where the first fire was lit in October 1970. For the purposes of this explanation, the carbon-bake furnace can be regarded as a series of pits surrounded by brick-built flues through which passes liquefied petroleum gas in a state of combustion on being mixed with air and ignited. Heat generated in the flues passes through the brickwork to heat up the contents of these open-topped pits. In the baking process, the pits are filled with carbon electrode blocks, newly produced from the green mill. In the newly produced condition, these are described as 'green blocks' because, having not yet been baked, they are still relatively soft. In the baking process the volatile content of the liquid-pitch binder is driven off, leaving behind a hard, dense carbon electrode block. These blocks are stacked in rows of four wide five deep and surrounded and covered by petroleum coke dust. The purpose of the coke is to support the electrode blocks during baking. In this process they reach a high temperature in excess of 1100°C. Also the blocks in the topmost layer are insulated from oxidation due to contact with the atmosphere.

The process of starting up the bake furnace consists, then, of filling the open pits with a mixture of coke and blocks so as to absorb the heat progressively generated in the flues as combustion increasingly takes place. To begin with, because of the cold and somewhat damp condition of the newly-built refractory pits or linings of the vast concrete tank in which the pits have been built, it is not so much a question of building up temperature as drying out the brickwork. This is a process which continues for some two weeks. After that the temperature very slowly builds up until, after about eight weeks, baking temperature conditions are reached. Although each baking furnace consists in our case of some sixty-four cells and each cell of five pits, the furnace remains static. As many as four combustion zones may be used at a time. In operating the furnace the combustion zone is moved progressively from cell to cell so that the contents of the pits are progressively warmed up and cooled down after baking as the fire or combustion zone passes by. This is done by moving the gas burners' firing manifold once every day and, similarly, moving the extraction manifold which removes the products of combustion. For the first few days, maintaining adequate draught and achieving steady burning conditions involved continuous activity on the part of the maintenance millwrights, particularly in the first few hours.

Of all the start-up activities taking place in 1970–71, the bake was probably the most straightforward and satisfactory. Of course, the operation of much of the mechanical equipment mounted on the high duty overhead cranes did not come into use until, with the furnaces having reached operating temperature, it was time to start removing the start-up contents and to begin loading green blocks in earnest. This began towards the end of January 1970. By April, substantial quantities of baked anodes were emerging from the bake furnace and piling up in the baked-block store at the end of that building.

Green mill start-up

The green mill in the carbon plant did not start operation until late in December 1970. It could not be regarded as achieving satisfactory operation, even on low output, until February or March 1971. The bake furnace had been started up earlier in order to be ready to receive green carbon blocks towards the end of 1970, at which time there would have been an overrun of some ten weeks against the original construction programme. This was due largely to delays in the summer of 1970 in the completion of erection followed by extended delays in the commissioning period.

While some of these problems can fairly be described as farcical, such as the inability of one elevator to lift the majority of the material fed into it and deliver it at the point of discharge, this difficulty persisted for some two or three months. On the other hand, a particularly good job was done in commissioning the exceedingly complex green mill control-room panel in something like three months from start to finish. It should be explained that the heart of the green mill consists of a large console in which all the individual pieces of equipment and their operating status are indicated on a mimic diagram. The indication lights and symbols are coloured so that the operator can tell at a glance what is going on. More than that, this one man can feed carbon in the appropriate quantities and sizes to the batch mixers together with weighed-out quantities of liquid pitch binder. This produces controlled mixed carbon paste at the end of a one-hour mixing cycle for feeding to the electrode presses in which the green electrode blocks are produced. These processes are carried out in a number of sequentially linked trains of equipment. Whilst each unit of plant can be started and stopped individually from the control room, each train can also be operated in sequence.

Located immediately behind the control panel itself is a motor-control centre in which all the motor-control gear, complete with individual protective equipment and inter-connecting wiring, is sited. To and from this connections lead to the actual drives at the appropriate point in this 190-foot-tall building. Not only did this electrical equipment comprise and embrace the usual features to ensure that each individual drive was protected from overload from whatever reason, and was inter-connected with the preceding and succeeding drives in any given train, but a variety of interlocks were provided to ensure that mechanical and electrical damage did not result from any malfunction. Inevitably, such a complex set of interlocking systems proved extremely difficult to commission. It was no small achievement to complete the process commissioning of the green mill control facilities in some twelve weeks.

Rodding room start-up

The rodding room is the building in which the electrical conductors are fitted to the holes provided for the purpose in the uppermost surfaces of the baked-carbon electrode blocks. These conductors consist of aluminium hanger bars friction-welded at their lower end to nine-inch diameter steel stubs which are cast into the carbon block by a cast-clay poured cast-iron joint. This process is carried out on a turntable or carousel machine whereby the block and hangers are matched up together at one station, then brought around to the cast-iron pouring station before offloading under the control of the operator who initiates an otherwise automatic discharging system. This particular operation is but one of a long sequence carried out on electrodes returning after use in the reduction process. The process leads through a series of stages in which the individual components are prepared for re-use, followed by the casting operation and eventual shipment over to the cell rooms. In between each operation, the electrodes are carried out on an overhead monorail conveyor system.

Each operation was commissioned by itself but, of course, in the production process, the operation has to proceed continuously and in sequence. Initially a considerable amount of trouble was experienced with each of the operations but increasingly, as load built up, a much more fundamental set of problems was encountered because of the sequential layout of the system. In other words, a breakdown at any point in the chain brought the entire conveyor system to a halt. At first, in the spring of 1971, the cast-iron melting furnaces were satisfactorily put to work. Not without difficulty the casting turntable was brought into use. The conveyor system required structural strengthening. The thimble press for removing the used cast-iron joints started to work satisfactorily. The stub shotblasting equipment worked well. So, too, did the butt shotblasting equipment. Probably the greatest difficulty was experienced with the butt crusher. This is in fact a horizontally-mounted hydraulic press whose main duty is to remove the remains of the carbon electrode following the end of its useful life in the reduction cell. The unit is returned to the rodding room so that its hanger assembly can be re-used. There was no difficulty about the hydraulic motion. But there was in satisfactorily crushing a full-size block (the only kind of electrode available) without damaging the cast-iron joint and thereby feeding the carbon plant with a steady supply of unwanted large pieces of cast-iron mixed up with returning scrap carbon. That apart, the commissioning of the rodding room was relatively painless.

Reduction start-up

However, the big event towards which everything else had been directed and which was the focus of great excitement was the planned start-up of the reduction cell room due for later in the spring. This was set for 1 May 1971. It was attended by Mr R. E. Utiger, managing director of BA, Mr D. P. Keller, director of reduction, and about two dozen men seconded for a short period from Reynolds Metals Company to help in the start-up. For many of them, this was the latest in a series of start-ups or re-starts. Reduction cells were to be started in rooms 1 and 2, originally known as pot rooms 50 and 52. Thirty-two cells (the first two sections) in each room were to be started, making a total of sixty-four in all. This number was determined by the minimum operating voltage of the rectifier equipment. The supervision of the start-up would be in the hands of a shift superintendent assisted by two room supervisors, these men being recruited and trained for the purpose by BA. However, during the start-up there would be a senior Reynolds general foreman assigned to each shift together with two experienced RMC foremen working in each room. This added up to five RMC men on each shift, making a total of twenty. On each shift two room supervisors came over from the States for the first three weeks of the start-up only. The senior man and the other two supervisors remained for a further three weeks. Within two months only a handful were left. One man, Jay Domenico, remained until the end of the year.

Little mention has been made in describing the start-up arrangement in other departments of the contribution made by RMC personnel. They did, of course, make a major contribution to design and construction, both at Southall and on site. Then in providing assistance to the operating management, RMC personnel came over to the carbon plant in 1970. Thus Jack Sulton and Walt Strauss were present throughout, as was Tex Hayes for the green mill and bake start-up. Jerry Glidewell having finished his construction duties, was a major participant in the rodding room start-up. But far and away the biggest impact and the most immediate and direct contribution to start-up was the presence of the twenty experienced RMC men. Just as well, because it very soon became apparent that sixty-four cells were too many to start from cold without facilities for the production of liquid flux. Much heat was generated and much hard and unpleasant work was carried out before, early on the morning of Thursday, 5 May 1971, Tom Dingwall was able to cut in cell 108 and make the first aluminium at Invergordon. By that time it had been necessary temporarily to cut out about half the sixty-four cells which had been brought on load and which had been standing at high temperature since the Monday evening. By transferring flux as it melted, the remaining cells were successively brought into circuit and, in about two weeks from Saturday, 1 May, sixty-four cells were in operation and the reduction department had grown up overnight.

The technique used in bringing the first sixty-four cells into use was what is known as a resistor grist start; that is to say, before electrical power is applied to the circuit, a layer of coke is laid between the anode and cathode electrodes in each cell. The purpose of this is to create a conducting path for direct electrical current from the anode to the cathode of sufficiently high resistance to generate heat and thereby slowly bring the entire electrode assembly system up to something approaching operating temperature. Once sufficiently high temperature is reached, it is possible to insulate each reduction cell by applying solid cryolite around the sides and ends, thereby confining the heat to the current path between the electrodes. As the cryolite warms up, it begins to melt out and eventually a pool of conducting flux is formed on the cathode immediately below the anode system and, of course, the resistor grist remains floating in the electrolyte.

One of the disadvantages of this method is that it is dirty. Once the cell is in full commission there is much hot arduous work to be undertaken in cleaning away the resistor grist which has not been oxidized or otherwise removed. When sufficient liquid electrolyte has been created or added to each reduction cell, alumina is added to the top surfaces and gradually dissolved in the electrolyte. Whereupon the process of electrolytic reduction begins. In the early stages this is thermally inefficient, somewhat unstable in electrical and physical terms. The process of bringing a reduction cell into a normal operating state occupies a matter of days in which various adjustments are made which might include the introduction of liquid metal in order to create a heat sink so as to bring down the temperature of the electrolyte. All these various operations are carried on in parallel, as they uniquely are during the start-up of a large number of cells. These activities occupied the first two weeks in May. Towards the end of May it was encouraging to find that the particular design of the reduction cell in use at Invergordon was proving to be stable and even docile. True, the sides of the reduction cell cavities had been heavily oxidized during the early stages of commissioning but, in the first weeks of life, this did not constitute a serious difficulty. However, the intention had originally been to cut in, as the process of starting up is know, 160 cells comprising line 1 within some six to eight weeks. For various reasons, it was to take more than twice as long, or 20 weeks to be precise.

In June 1971 a further thirty-two cells (those in sections 3 in rooms 2 and 2 of line 1) were cut in. The cut-in itself was fairly normal inasmuch as there was ample liquid flux (as the electrolyte is known) available for transfer to the cells which could be started at approximately daily intervals. This operation was carried out under much better control than the initial start-up of sections 1 and 2. However, in mid-June there were two bouts of serious difficulty with the electrical power installation. The electrical power as used in the electrolytic reduction process is, of course, direct current which has been rectified from the alternating current of the incoming power supply. The incoming power supply is also delivered at high tension. The first stage of conversion for use into direct current involves transforming the electrical voltage from 132000 volts or 275000 volts down to 33000. At this voltage the power is supplied to the rectifier station in which alternating current is converted to direct current at a maximum circuit voltage of 750. Difficulties arose in the rectifier units. Six so-called rectiformers had been installed for each reduction cell line and, of these six, five had the designed rated capacity to support the full reduction load at 130000 amps. The trouble took the form of a failure of the protective fuses on the rectifier units themselves, each rectifier consisting of a number of stacks of individual rectification diodes, each diode being protected by its own fuse and, as each fuse failed, so the load on each unit was transferred to the remaining units. Consequently, failure occurred at an increasingly rapid rate, leading to the ultimate failure of each unit. These fuses were quite large, expensive, and took considerable time to install, an operation which was not easy – the initial difficulties took the form of replacing fuses until such time as the root cause of the trouble had been diagnosed. Eventually the problem was solved by increasing the fuse rating and by adding one additional diode to each stack. Thus, by the end of June, this particular bout of trouble had been overcome.

However, in the process, the reduction cells had been subjected to several reductions in line current which resulted in a reduction of the heat input. It will be appreciated that the thermal equilibrium of a reduction cell is a vital operating parameter and, in order that it be maintained in a stable state in the event of line current being

E

reduced, it is necessary to increase the voltage. This process of reduction in heat and increase power input tends to have a damaging effect and is, of course, a source of all kinds of operating difficulties for process operators, supervision and management. Extra fume is generated, extra work caused and there is uncertainty about the exact levels of the voltage and current which should be applied and to the additions of solid electrolyte and alumina which are appropriate to the particular situation. More than that, it is very often almost impossible for the maintenance engineering department to predict the likely duration of such unstable and uncertain conditions. So it was with a sense of relief that it was believed that, by the end of June 1971, these teething troubles, as they were seen, had been overcome in the rectifier installation. The way was now clear for a further increase in load from July onwards. However, in the meantime, problems had arisen elsewhere.

While output from the green mill was no higher than necessary to support the limited number of cells in circuit due, for instance, to the fact that only one anode press out of the two to be installed was available for production use, in the baking furnace the problem was that of process control. Water had penetrated into some parts of the baking furnace and, as a result, blocks were emerging with oxidized carbon bottoms. On introduction to the reduction cell, this soft carbon became dislodged, gave rise to further work, generated extra heat, wasted power and created other attendant difficulties in the reduction department. The process of eliminating this trouble took the form of pumping out water and reducing the water table in the area surrounding the bake, for which purpose pumping units had been installed before commencement. Attention was also paid to other aspects of the baking process to ensure that all blocks were satisfactorily baked and emerged as hard, good electrical conductors according to specification. Substantially this was overcome by early August but not before a great deal of carbon had appeared in the reduction cells, causing alarm and consternation. The early indications had been that, whatever the difficulties with rectifiers and reduction cells, at least a good carbon anode had been and was being produced.

Also in the carbon plant, the rodding room, with all its mechanical complexity, was proving unreliable, maintenance-intensive and difficult to control and manage. Production was erratic and the supply of sufficient rodded anodes to maintain more than the ninety-six cells commissioned by July was in serious doubt. Indeed, production management was reluctant to proceed with the commissioning of the remaining eighty-four cells. Nevertheless, because of the major effort applied both in engineering and production management in the carbon plant, as a result of information gleaned from method studies of process and engineering bottlenecks, the decision was taken to proceed with the commissioning of further cells. Fortunately, it proved that not only did carbon quality increasingly reach a satisfactory level, but the rodding room difficulties, which were to persist for several years, were overcome to the extent that one line (half of the total plant installed capacity) could be supported by the autumn of 1971. Through August and September, the remaining eighty-four reduction cells were commissioned.

Beginning with cells 149, 150 and 151, an attempt was made to introduce the so-called metal bake start. In this process, instead of resistor grist, liquid aluminium is poured into the reduction cell in which it immediately freezes before subsequent gradual melting out through the heating effect of the electric current. While this is a method which had proved successful with the commissioning of large Soderberg reduction cells in the United States, it proved to be difficult to apply to the eighteen-anode pre-bake cell more recently developed and installed at Invergordon. It was very difficult to ensure that equal current sharing was being achieved between each of the anodes. In the absence of a good current distribution, it was all too easy to cause overheating and failure of the anode to carbon joint. These failures were explosive, quite alarming, and potentially dangerous to the unwary. Although a number of people literally lost their shirts, no one was seriously injured. The method was used extensively in commissioning the remaining cells in line 1 to a satisfactorily reliable state. So much for the reduction start-up in 1971.

Engineering

The engineering function was late in formation for a number of reasons. For one thing, it was essential to find an experienced engineer to take charge of the function. For another, it was important not to attempt to carry out design and planning or organization and other aspects appropriate to this department until the engineering manager had taken up his appointment. This did not happen, in fact, until February 1970. Even at that relatively late date, late by comparison with personnel and production functions, the incumbent was still distracted by substantial involvement in the design and construction activities which were clearly a matter of great personal interest to the man himself and of great future significance to the operating management and, in particular, his own function.

Consequently, senior department heads of the constituent parts of the engineering function were late in appointment as were the subordinate area engineers. Remembering that, as early as June 1970, recruitment of hourly-paid employees, including maintenance craftsmen, was under way, this meant that the entire engineering nucleus was formed and brought into operation in some three to four months. This was not long enough. The consequences remained with the function and the plant for several years and, indeed, throughout its formative stage: a number of organizational concepts and other philosophical or conceptual aspects of operating management policy and procedure were already well advanced. These were matters in which the late-arriving engineers had taken no part. Consequently, they had to undergo study and familiarization programmes in order to become acquainted with the state which had been reached in planning the management procedure and practices. Not all of these were easy to assimilate or, indeed, entirely acceptable to the newly-arriving engineers, whose numbers seemed to increase week by week. There was no time to re-evaluate and revise. It was very difficult to gather groups of people together in order to thrash out the reasons for many of the decisions which had already been taken and to persuade the newcomers of their validity. Equally, it was difficult to find the time for those familiarization tours of other reduction plants which had been such a feature of the early study and planning work on the part of production personnel and senior management. This delay is a subject which would warrant careful study on the part of any organization contemplating any future development like the Invergordon smelter.

Clearly, identity of outlook and compatibility of behaviour are essential if any management team wishes to function as a cohesive unit. Some of the frictions and mistakes, difficulties which arose as the inevitable conflicts of interest emerged between functions as the plant settled down to work were due not so much to role conflict as to an incomplete understanding or lack of acceptance of policies thrashed out among the other departments which had long come to accept them and identify with them. Nevertheless, the engineering function, as it came together, did embody several striking departures from traditional plant engineering organizations. For one thing, cratfsmen were to be grouped according to three skilled trades – mechanical, electrical and building. There were to be no turners or riggers or welders or welder burners or fitters' mates, but multi-skilled mechanical craftsmen. The intention was to recruit time-served craftsmen and to arrange the necessary supplementary training so that a skilled machinist could learn – if he did not already know – supplementary skills of rigging, bench-fitting and so on. Similarly, vehicle mechanics were to receive training in rigging, machining and so on. Similarly, electrical craftsmen were to be capable of working on any piece of electrical equipment throughout the plant, save only one area – that of the high-tension switchyard where only those who had passed through a NOSHEB high-tension training course and duly certificated as having passed at the necessary standard would be admitted to work. Again, building trades workers were to be trained to the necessary standards of skill required in the trades of bricklaying, joinery, painting, fence repair and so on.

Another prime difference lay in the absence of the conventional foreman and chargehand supervisory position recruited exclusively from time-served craftsmen. On the contrary, it was believed that technically qualified supervisory engineers should take charge of the appropriate squad of multi-skilled craftsmen based at or having responsibility for a section of the plant. The plant was divided into areas and placed under the charge of an area engineer, each of whom had the appropriate allocation of mechanical, electrical and building trades craftsmen. The area engineers were responsible to mechanical, electrical or building superintendents who, in turn, answered to the engineering manager.

To mention only one more major difference, but perhaps the most important, complete flexibility between crafts was achieved from the beginning. That is to say in any sequential operation maintenance task it was not necessary for an electrician to disconnect a piece of apparatus and call for a fitter or rigger to remove it to the workshop, whereafter only an electrician could open up an electric motor, followed by mechanical and separate electrical examination and inspection. Such a sequence is a common feature throughout British industry and is normally accompanied by a time delay between each successive stage which extends, particularly in the case of continuous operating plants, for a period far longer than the aggregate of the individual working times on each sub-task. The result is that the downtime on the plant can very often reach three to five times the length of that achievable by the same craftsmen working successively or of one craftsman working continuously. It is interesting to note that both the craftsmen originally recruited had been made clearly aware of the policy which was to be applied. Their successors have found, and continue to find, increased satisfaction and very few practical difficulties in the application of this system.

The engineering function took over a barely-completed workshop, a plant full of partially-completed and partially-commissioned plant equipment and a drawing office without any drawings or records. All the drawings, schedules, specifications, catalogues and all the other paraphernalia which is the bread and butter of any maintenance engineering organization were still in the hands of BA and TWW construction personnel. The hand-over was gradual and rarely easy, seldom complete. Even when complete, maintenance instructions and the carefully ordered spare parts were rarely to be found intact. For the next eighteen months the engineering personnel lived hand-to-mouth. It is to their credit that the difficulties which they encountered did not result in even more serious delays and difficulties than were, in fact, their lot.

Casthouse start-up

The casthouse equipment was more or less complete in May 1971. However, the only metal-handling trials which had been carried out using ingots imported from other BA plants had been involved in the proving of weighbridge and other mechanical handling equipment. Such metal as had been melted in the new holding furnaces was only available for casting in a very tiny rotary ingot-casting machine. This was a very clever machine of the daisy-wheel pattern involving internal mould cooling. In the dry-run testing which was carried out, it performed perfectly under load and, as the heat of the metal being cast increasingly raised the temperature of the moulds and other equipment, difficulties began to accumulate until it was eventually discarded as a production machine. The importance of this should not be exaggerated inasmuch as its purpose had been to provide the means of casting so-called hardeners. These are alloys of aluminium with other metals such as iron, copper, magnesium, or whatever, and are used in blending with metal from the reduction cells in order to form the commercial alloys cast for subsequent use by rolling mills and extrusion plants.

In mid-May 1971 the first blocks were cast in the vast twenty-foot-deep vertical direct-chill casting machines which formed the principal equipment of this very large casting shop. The casting shop was a very close replica of the casting shop built by Reynolds Metals in their extension to the Longview smelter in 1967 and 1968, and that was a good casting plant. The vertical D C machines and their attendant pair of 90000 lb capacity holding furnaces along with their control equipment should, therefore, have been a straightforward repeat of something which had been built before and proved successful in operation. Alas, it was not to be. Not only were the control installations very quickly to prove unreliable (and one memorable cast was completed without any instrumentation and with some doubt as to the cooling water supply – an extremely dangerous undertaking) but, in addition, the top and bottom hardware which is a permanent fixture in each casting machine proved to be unique to each machine rather than interchangeable. Similarly, the installation and transfer of moulds for the appropriate ingots and shapes to be cast proved to be unique to each machine. Two vital degrees of interchangeability which had been achieved at Longview were not achieved by those installing the equipment at Invergordon. Small wonder that the frustration of the casthouse production staff with both construction and maintenance engineers gave rise to severe friction throughout the summer and autumn of 1971.

However, if the difficulties with the vertical casting were tried and proved slow to overcome, they were as nothing by comparison with the difficulties experienced in commissioning the horizontal casting machine. However, inasmuch as the demand for its production and its rated output were both relatively low, its significance in the history of the casting shop was limited. Along with the dross recovery and hardener casting installations, these ancillary systems were jettisoned in the casting shop at the end of 1971. It would be wrong to say that the problems associated with these sub-systems had been fully overcome by 1975. It is probably true that, in this area, the detailed engineering was less successful than in any other part of the smelter.

Materials handling

This is the name given to the department responsible for literally handling incoming materials and outgoing products. With the smelter was associated a 3300-foot-long pier extending from the shore at the village of Saltburn out into the Cromarty Firth. This pier carried not only a roadway but a four-foot-wide cable belt conveyor system. This conveyor was intended to handle alumina at a rate of up to 1500 tonnes per hour from self-unloading bulk carrier vessels which would bring alumina direct from overseas sources, mostly in Jamaica, to the Invergordon pier. As cargo sizes would normally be of the order of 30000 to 35000 tonnes, the expectation that a vessel would be unloaded and turned around in well under three days seemed reasonable. It was not so easy to achieve but, nevertheless, the unloading of the first cargo in January 1971, extending as it did to nine days and involving numerous adjustments to the belt and cable system, proved to be by far the worst ship-unloading experienced. Progressively time was reduced until, in early 1972, such cargoes were being unloaded in some sixty-odd hours elapsed time.

Of course, the materials handling department was also responsible for bringing in supplies of petroleum coke, cryolite and aluminium fluoride. They usually arrived in palletized, bagged form, at the pier where they were unloaded from coastal vessels by means of a 50-tonne crane provided for the purpose. The coke was handled by the belt conveyor system up to the junction tower in the plant from which the material, be it alumina or coke, was diverted under the control of a single operator to the appropriate storage silo. Palletized material was taken by truck to the plant and stored ready for use in the warehouse provided for the purpose. Other incoming material included liquid pitch. This again was a self-unloading process whereby the pitch tanker driver dumped his cargo into an underground storage tank from where it was pumped into the tanks feeding the circulating ring main just out-side the carbon plant green mill.

Another large volume of incoming material was liquefied petroleum gas (LPG.) This material came by 250-tonne train loads of tank cars from Grangemouth or Stanlow which were unloaded at a specially designed and installed gantry in three to four hours. Although this was a particularly intricate system, fully equipped with automatic sprays in order to minimize the danger of fire out-break (complying in full with the stringent regulations devised for the storage and handling of this material), no serious difficulty was experienced in commissioning it and bringing it into use. Storage capacity consisted of two 750-tonne Horton spheres stationed on the east boundary of the plant. In order to bring in LPG and to remove cargoes of outgoing cast aluminium products, a rail spur extension had been built into the smelter dividing just inside the perimeter to the LPG area on the one hand and to the casthouse on the west face of the plant on the other. A rail-loading dock extended inside the casthouse, enabling metal to be lifted direct from the block and billet-sawing stations by overhead crane and placed into empty rail cars previously positioned in rail loading docks.

Beyond this, of course, materials handling had a miscellaneous range of responsibilities for storage, reception and clearance of a wide variety of materials and objects originating from every part of the plant.

Other departments

In some ways the most delicate and intricate start-ups occurred not amongst the heavy concentrations of engineering equipment but in the chemical laboratory and in the medical centre. Yet, apart from initial and protracted difficulties in securing precisely the right equipment required for the multiple tasks and operations required in these areas, once the materials had been delivered and the installation was fully completed, these areas provided less difficulty than many of those in which vast experience had been accumulated elsewhere.

Here again, it is interesting to speculate as to why this should have been so. While the particular processes of chemical analysis had been in use in reduction plants for many years, the Inver-

E*

gordon laboratory, developed from the installation at Longview, was one of the most highly-mechanized laboratories in the aluminium industry. Yet both in terms of its ability to handle the volume of samples for analysis and in terms of accuracy of its analyses, no serious problems were ever encountered. Quite the reverse: in all the inter-laboratory checks which were progressively instituted through 1971 and 1972, in no single case was the Invergordon laboratory ever faulted in either respect. Indeed, in these checks, on several occasions other well-established and well-managed laboratories were found to be in minor respects less accurate and reliable than the new unit at Invergordon.

Similarly, the medical centre, complete with its emergency reception ward including basic operating facilities, X-ray room, physiotherapy room, doctor's surgery and audiometric testing room (to mention only the major facilities provided) went to work. Although, mercifully, not too heavily occupied in its early months it was soon providing a seven-day, twenty-four-hour service embracing not only treatment of injuries and of those taken sick while at work but progressively moving into preventive medicine.

In both cases, the laboratory and the medical centre had been the subject of the most elaborate and detailed planning and scheduling, both as to the architectural layout and detailed design of each room, purpose-built for its function, and as to the meticulous specification of equipment and materials to be supplied and used by those responsible for running the department. All of this was pursued, negotiated and discussed over some two years. The moral would seem to be something to do with knowing what you want and knowing it when you see it and also knowing the genuine article.

12 Completion and Consolidation

Smelter operation

By September 1971 the smelter was operating at half its rated capacity and output was held at that level for some time to come. Market demand had begun to fall in 1970 and the intention to restrict operations at Invergordon to half capacity was announced in April 1971 at a press conference held at the plant. It would be misleading to suggest that this was other than a very welcome relief to the operating staff who had just been through an unnecessarily trying nine months in which all departments had to overcome not only the frustrations inseparable from large-scale plant commissioning but also a number of difficulties which should not have occurred at all. Nevertheless, as the autumn of 1971 deepened into winter, operating performance results began to improve. In January 1972 they reached levels of efficiency very much better than had ever been forecast. This was true both as to power consumption and metal purity and the future looked extremely promising. More than that, although the experience of 1971 had been serious and damaging, none of the problems encountered had been fundamental, disastrous or irreparable. As the history of the aluminium industry has included not a few disastrous episodes in the design and start-up of reduction plants, the possibility that it might happen again is an ever-present nightmare at the back of the minds of those directly involved. Fortunately, the symptoms of serious trouble are readily identifiable and appear early. Consequently, even by Christmas 1971 it was reassuringly clear that, whatever worries and doubts there might be, stark disaster was not in view. Or so it was thought.

Power failure

At 0338 hours on Friday, 21 January 1972, widespread failure of power supplies occurred throught the north-east of Scotland. That is the time when all power supplies to the smelter failed although, no doubt, the large-scale grid failure had its origin in the inability of the power system to cope with bad weather conditions which caused a build-up of ice on high-tension cables carrying power over relatively remote and exposed parts of the country. The NOSHEB power-distribution system is monitored and controlled by the staff at the central control room at Port-na-Craig near Pitlochry. Like the smelter itself, the CCR is constantly manned, and there is direct telephonic communication between the two. With emergency lighting in use, CCR advised the smelter during the first hour of total shutdown that they hoped to restore power in about half an hour and, in the cell rooms, the unusual quiet was interrupted occasionally by subdued plops, hisses and bubbles as the molten contents of all 160 cells began to solidify. As the minutes passed and senior staff arrived by car, it became apparent that the brown-out extended from Aberdeen in the south to the Dornoch Firth in the north, beyond which smelter staff leaving their homes in Tain could see lights as usual. After numerous and increasingly alarmed telephone calls with NOSHEB staff and by dint of their efforts in what must have been an unprecedented situation because of the size of the power loads to be handled, power supplies were eventually restored after an interruption of two and three-quarter hours.

While power supplies were being progressively restored throughout the north-east counties, the smelter experienced further short-duration interruptions but, by the time senior BA executives in London were being awakened by telephone calls from the north, effective stability had been achieved. But there remained the daunting prospect of restoring thermal and electrical balance to the reduction cells. Night-shift personnel were asked to work a consecutive day-shift. They agreed to do so in anticipation of the trouble to come. And come it did. The uneven current distribution among the anode assemblies, caused by the absence of power which had created partial solidification and, hence, irregular resistance, inevitably resulted in the unpredictable failure of some stub-to-carbon joints. In all, there were about 110 'burn-offs', as these failures are called. When a burn-off occurs, the carbon electrode is left resting on the cathode cell bottom immersed in molten electrolyte which makes it hot and 'soapy'. As a new electrode weighs 625 Kg or some 1100 lb, removal of a burn-off is a difficult and thoroughly unpleasant task involving the use of eight-foot-long tongs suspended from the 50-tonne crane. To complete the removal of over 110 burn-offs in some sixteen hours was a remarkable achievement by the cell-room personnel, testifying to their guts and dedication. Even so, four cells were cut out of operation before an open circuit occurred, because of the dangerous implications of any such event for people and their equipment. So the smelter survived without permanent damage but it was an experience verging on the terrifying for those actively involved. Within a week or two most people had drawn breath and regained confidence. Here, however, was another experience which did more harm than good and from which only the most sombre conclusions could be drawn.

Power restriction

Only a few weeks later, notice was served on the smelter that a deliberate reduction in load must be carried out as part of a nation-wide campaign to conserve energy for essential purposes. In the outcome, 64 cells out of a total of 160 in use were taken out of circuit – a heartbreaking task for those who had first started them up six months earlier and re-started them only the month before. By March 1972 this emergency had passed and the laborious task of re-starting began again. Advantage was taken of the limited re-start rate to carry out repairs to the cathode side linings. By June 1972 the smelter had been restored to 50% of rated capacity.

Personnel policies in practice

Meanwhile the oil-related construction industries had moved into Easter Ross with Brown and Root (UK) Ltd in collaboration with George Wimpey & Co. Ltd developing a large site at Nigg and MK-Shand taking an initial lease of fity acres of land owned by BA adjacent to the smelter itself behind the village of Saltburn. To begin with, much of the activity was concerned with site preparation and facility construction but by September 1972 recruitment of permanent work forces had begun. By the end of 1972, all surplus housing had been soaked up and the start-up of line 2 at the smelter, justified by the emerging boom of 1973–74, began against a background of increasing difficulty in recruitment and retaining manpower at the smelter. The story of the implications of running the smelter in the face of the problems posed by rapid development of the oil-related construction industries is part of the history of the whole Moray Firth area, in which the smelter's experiences were not disparate from those of other existing industries. Certainly, if there is a lesson to be learned, it is that manpower and infrastructure planning are indivisible.

During the period extending from June 1970 until the end of 1972 there was ample experience of operation in all departments by which to assess the manpower planning which preceded it. Recruitment, selection and training could each be tested against performance in practice; so could manning levels and productivity performance. Indeed the entire management philosophy and the whole apparatus of software, hardware and manpower had been stressed to a degree scarcely anticipated and certainly not in the ways expected. Industrial relations policy and organizational structure had both been in use over a lengthy period in which they had been affected in different ways.

Recruitment and selection were self-evidently effective after early and relatively minor modifications to the practices adopted. As time went on, further experiences corroborated the belief (that standards should be developed from first principles and maintained consistently as a basis for training and actual motivation) in a selective approach as valid. No evidence emerged to suggest that it would have been better to cream off the labour population, i.e. to select the most intelligent or physically most robust applicants for each job. The questions to be asked in answer to the question, 'Why not just employ the best applicants?' must surely be, 'By what criteria do you measure "best"? What does "best" specifically mean in any given context?' Nor did any evidence emerge before the end of 1972 to show that it would have been wiser or more advantageous to take the applicants on a 'run of the market' basis and put them to work after minimal (say one week) training. All experience of 1971–72 confirmed that the deliberate choice of the particular recruitment, selection and training policies and practices had been conspicuously wise.

Manning levels, on the other hand, had been underestimated in both engineering and reduction departments. Engineering manpower was to increase progressively as the smelter came on to full operation, reflecting a number of unpredicted areas of equipment reliability. In the reduction department the original crew level for each cell room had been synthesized to six men although in optimum circumstances at steady state five men would suffice. But in the outcome it was found necessary to increase the number to seven in October 1971. The number was based on the allocation of five men to cell operation (sixteen cells/man), one man driving the 50-tonne crane and one man assisting in the several two-man operations, such as tapping or blocking. However, flexibility was established in practice and proved invaluable. Elsewhere manning levels had to be adjusted upwards. There is little doubt, though, that the increases would have been greater still but for the detailed knowledge of work load as planned and as observed in actuality. Even so, the total increase in full operation over the 1967 feasibility study level did not exceed one-third although a number of base changes had occurred.

Productivity was exceptional as to effort, particularly during the various crises. Flexibility was achieved, it is worth repeating, in all departments. The reservations to be entered related to equipment damage and safe working practices, the importance of which was difficult to sustain in emergencies and to re-establish afterwards. This seemed to go hand-in-hand with the adaptability which flexibility required and which recruits from forestry and agricultural backgrounds brought with them in contrast to those from occupations in military or Government service. In this experience, Invergordon replicated that of several Scandinavian smelters where similar transfers occurred.

The management philosophy was obviously acceptable to most employees as to what is now called harmonization, the absence or elimination of social or status differentiations. As to the development of any identity with the company or even what might be called the external fortunes of the smelter (the use made by customers of products and the state of trade) this was largely absent, as was the presence of any positive wish to be consulted on any non-wage-related or non-disciplinary matter.

Housing

The earliest estimates of housing requirements were based on the original BA feasibility study in which it was concluded that 650 full-time employees would be required to operate the smelter. After making allowances for recruitment of people who were already housed within travelling distance of the smelter and for a supply of private housing, it was concluded that 312 houses would be required to provide rented accommodation for the balance of smelter employees. This figure formed the basis of housing and infrastructure planning by the local authorities and was not adjusted when the first estimate of total employee strength was produced by the operating management in April 1969. The new figure of 550 was based on a number of assumptions as to the likely product mix, method of metal shipment, extent and severity of plant and equipment problems to be overcome initially, flexibility of manpower utilization possible with high degree of mechanization, and so on. It was an estimate of what could be achieved, other things being equal, and was based on carefully synthesized data collected from plant design information and visits to existing plants already in operation. Even by early 1971, this figure had only increased to 585 as a result of some assumptions being modified in the light of more realistic and reliable information becoming available. By that time recruitment was well under way and it was evident that more employees would be recruited from the area surrounding the smelter than had been expected. The estimate of housing units likely to be taken up by smelter employees was thereupon revised downwards to 280 in spite of the increased number of jobs being filled. In fact, this was further revised towards the end of 1971, downwards again to 234 in view of the continuing high proportion of recruits of local residence. This led to a substantial number of houses standing empty (although the full economic rent was being paid to the housing authority by BA in fulfilment of its original commitment). This, in turn, exposed the County Council to increasing criticism on the grounds that too many houses had been built. This criticism was most vocal in the spring of 1972 when the recession in demand for aluminium was at its nadir and was possibly exacerbated by the conclusion of negotiations between BA and the County Council in April 1972 which resulted in forty houses available to BA employees being opened to general housing list applicants and the company ceasing to pay rent for those forty vacant houses.

As was pointed out at the time, oil-related industrial development had already begun in Easter Ross and was soon to expand rapidly. The housing authority was thus able to make good, early use of the returned houses. By September 1972 BA was regretting the decision to return the houses for, by this time, a long-term alumina-to-metal conversion contract had been signed which would guarantee an outlet for metal from the hitherto-idle line 2 at the smelter. Not only that but, after two years with minimal manpower wastage, the high wages paid by the oil-related construction industries were beginning to attract manpower from the smelter. This situation was to develop rapidly over the next two years but subsequent events could not detract from the fact that careful manpower planning enabled housing needs to be forecast accurately and provided in good time without penalty to the taxpayer. Had there been no oil-related development in Easter Ross, the vacant houses would all have been occupied before the end of 1972 by new recruits to the smelter.

Machinery and equipment

Leaving aside power supply interruptions attributable to external power restrictions or grid failures, many instances of equipment failure occurred within the smelter itself. These were numerous and widespread. A few examples will illustrate the diversity and severity of these instances.

In March 1971, an explosion occurred in a 625 hp, 3·3 KV. electric motor starter in the junction tower which destroyed the control gear and caused a dangerous fire. The equipment had been correctly installed and operated.

In June 1971, the first of two series of failures of the main power rectification equipment occurred, the second occurring some three weeks later. Both were serious and prolonged, resulting in emergency repair work being carried out day and night for several days on each occasion while cell rooms operated at reduced current and efficiency, generating excess heat and fume.

Previously, in April 1971, an 800 hp fume-extraction fan-drive motor exploded at night, sending pieces high into the air from which they fell to ground without, fortunately, injuring anyone. This was but one example of several repeated fan-drive failures in 1971 and later.

Induction furnaces supplied to the casthouse for special alloy hardener preparation or scrap re-melting purposes were installed with the wrong refractory material and to the wrong dimensions. Both later had to be shut down, dug out and re-lined twice.

Many more examples could be given of major equipment failures occurring early in the history of the plant and, doubtless, some incidence of such occurrences is inevitable at the birth of a large industrial complex. But the entire plant had been commissioned before or during hand-over to operating personnel. Both BA and TWW had not only themselves employed substantial numbers of commissioning or inspecting engineers but had also engaged a variety of independent specialists as well. How could so many such events occur in spite of such care and attention?

First, let it be said that these events represented a minority of the units in operation and many examples could be quoted of units exceeding designed performance. Secondly, several of the failures could not have been detected by any inspection or commissioning test in the unloaded condition where the fault lay in design concept and not in manufacture or site erection. Thirdly, some of the defects appeared as a result of the process of ageing through which all units would pass and, unless previously tried in service elsewhere, would be likewise undetectable on initial test. Fourthly, the sources of failure are in some cases unknown to this day.

Nevertheless, in the majority of cases failures occurred in units whose design was conservative and well within the limits prescribed by the state of the art. Very few of the comparatively small number of advanced technological applications gave any trouble in the outcome. None of the expected fears came true but too many failures occurred where no satisfactory explanation was forthcoming. Whether this experience is representative of major green field or capital expansion projects in this or other industries, it is hard to say. However, it is perfectly clear that such experience was largely avoidable – that it occurred on major units over the entire plant is a reflection on the heavy engineering industry and is inexcusable.

13 With Hindsight

The backdrop

The Invergordon smelter was built because in doing so the purposes of all interested parties coincided. It was explained in Chapter 3 that central Government was concerned to see an expansion of the primary aluminium industry and also to effect a significant measure of import substitution; Ross and Cromarty County Council was intent on achieving industrial development in Easter Ross and was equipped to do so. The Highlands and Islands Development Board was charged with improving the prosperity of the Highlands and Islands and so that of the remainder of the United Kingdom. The British Aluminium Company Limited itself had more than sufficient reason to build a major addition to its UK smelting capacity. Because there was this congruence of interests, the respective initiatives led to Government approval for the project with endorsement by all other parties and, also, by public opinion. Thus it was possible for private enterprise to act in concert with central and local government – as well as a number of other bodies – and, not only launch a major industrial project in the Highlands of Scotland but also bring it to a successful outcome. Such a result was not inevitable and several of the particular difficulties encountered have been mentioned previously. In recent experience other major projects of a similar kind have either failed to win general acceptance at the outset or, having been approved and authorized have failed at an early stage. If that statement merely reiterates a truism (more applicable to British industry than abroad, perhaps) that is too well known already, nevertheless there are relatively few documented accounts of the efforts made to succeed. News headlines and technological seminars, lectures and papers abound but in spite of – perhaps because of – a rather depressing record of project failure and technical development apparently foiled by 'poor industrial relations' the literature on these subjects is sparse indeed. The ability to learn from experience on 'green field site development' is limited by the scarcity of information as to what has been tried in the past and as to the result – not the overall result but the exact consequences of adopting particular policies and plans as to organization structure, personnel recruitment and training, manpower utilization, employee communication and motivation, learning and adaptive processes as well as a corresponding raft of plans and techniques in the fields of process technology, plant design, project financing, product marketing and so on.

Reasons for success and failure

1 The Invergordon smelter survived various birthpangs and vicissitudes before becoming established as a reliable contribution to the varied interests of its founding fathers in the mid-seventies. That it did so is therefore a source of satisfaction to those concerned and, no doubt others but, in addition, the satisfaction in whole or in part of particular interests must in some degree relate to the methods by which the project achieved success in particular respects and to varying degrees. Precisely because of the wide range of interests the verdicts on Invergordon could never be unanimous but it is worth enumerating a number of aspects in which success or failure may be identified with specific causes. The following aspects have been selected for illustrative purposes and are not, of course, comprehensive.

2 *Project management*
The smelter was built on time and within budget and this considerable achievement has been frequently reported elsewhere. That it was true in all respects (save some reservations that do not detract in substance) was probably due to technological competence, sound planning and effective project control. Because of a widely-share consensus as to the philosophy behind the process technology, the risk of failure in design, construction or commissioning was reduced. It was the belief of the nucleus of both project and operating managements that no radical innovations should be incorporated in fundamental design concepts but that the hardware should be such that well-known process techniques could be predictably and reliably implemented. It should not be thought that this implies mere reiteration of the tried and true for

many marginal but important refinements were incorporated in detailed design and the increase in unit sizes enabled economies of scale to be accomplished on the drawing board at least. In all these respects, success or failure depended on technological competence in design, construction as designed, satisfactory commissioning and effective utilization in operation. While generalization over a project as broad in its scope as any aluminium smelter must be of limited value, it would be fair to say that if design, construction and operation were on the whole effective, commissioning was not and under all four of these headings there were damaging exceptions. Design construction and commissioning of the rodding room was largely unsuccessful and, again, construction and commissioning of the casthouse left a great deal to be desired. Both were very late and incomplete. On the other hand cell room commissioning was good.

Project planning was not sophisticated and only simple techniques using bar charts and other diagrammatic methods were used. A critical path determination exercise was carried out in the spring of 1970 which served as a basis for planning by the operational management but it was not systematically updated. This was not in fact any handicap because the critical paths and unit completion dates did not change – acceleration of progress in order to meet these dates was crucial and obvious. In the main this was to be seen in round-the-clock working by commissioning and operating personnel until each task was nearly completed and in too many cases, equipment was handed over with a long list of minor defects and omissions awaiting rectification 'on-the-run' by operating personnel. However, this planning approach, enabling as it did firm executive control of site construction and commissioning progress to be carried out both by TWW and BA senior management was an important element in maintaining progress and recovering from setbacks. The unification of project management under TWW as directed by BA was an undoubted success in achieving virtual completion on time and within budget. If a different criterion was to be adopted – such as fault-free operation of all equipment under process operating conditions – a different view would hold but there are few circumstances in industry where such a criterion would be economically justifiable.

3   Buildings and equipment

The expeditious erection of buildings was a most impressive feature of construction work on site. Both foundations and floor placement in reinforced concrete and subsequent steel erection were carried out at a pace and to a quality standard rarely matched and seldom exceeded in the aluminium industry. The same could not be said of the design and construction of operating offices, mess-rooms and other service buildings which were often unready for occupation by operating personnel when required. This was an unnecessary disappointment often taken to reflect attitudes on the part of project management as to matters believed to be the prerogative of operating management given their economic insignificance.

Equipment was a very different matter. Only cell-room equipment was designed and built with the same flair that was evident in building construction. Across the plant, mechanical equipment and electrical services were the source of a great deal of unnecessary frustration, particularly in the commissioning stage. With the benefit of hindsight, more rigorous attitudes to design parameters and an insistence on performance equatable to the standards achieved in the major building should have been adopted and little extra cost would have resulted – indeed much subsequent operating expense would certainly have been saved.

4   Operating management

From process commissioning onwards a major dichotomy split operating management actual practices from planned intentions. While personnel recruitment and training was regarded by many visitors as having been carried out to an exceptionally high standard 'by the book', when the newly recruited personnel took over cranes with defective controls (such as long travel brakes) skills and attitudes induced by careful training and motivation were of less value than the ability to adapt and improvise. Here was a deep schism unfairly placed before operating personnel and, in particular, process supervisors and maintenance engineers. In the course of improvisation, much damage was done to equipment and buildings which could have been avoided. It was soon evident that process operators who had previously worked at sea or in agriculture or forestry could adapt more successfully in terms of accomplishing work stints than could those whose previous backgrounds lay in the military services or other well-regulated industries. But in doing so, equipment was abused and even when equipment became fully serviceable such habits persisted and remained in evidence for years to come.

In other respects, the operating management was successful in coping with the process start-ups and within nine months most departments had achieved levels of efficient performance on which the economic justification for investment in the plant then rested. Retrospectively it is evident that the engineering function was ill-prepared to meet a very different situation to that which had been expected. Production departments, in achieving performance too often did so at the expense of damage to buildings and equipment which resulted in a maintenance work load which saturated the tightly budgeted engineering capability. Any future project of this kind would obviously be well-advised to take a much more realistic view of the nature and magnitude of the total maintenance task on hand-over.

The other major problem area to confront operating management arose more slowly as the effects of long hours of work and frustrations increasingly became apparent within middle management. Here an interesting dilemma arises. Leaving aside the obvious need to handle the short term peak load hurdle occurring on plant take-over and start-up, there is an apparent need to avoid under-rating the lengthy subsequent working-up period as to burden on management. At the same time, extra management, engineering and supervisory personnel do not automatically lead to an acceleration in working-up and may not be easy to shed on completion. This is a subjective matter but it is suggested Invergordon was initially under-managed and subsequently it was decided to restructure management so as to limit work-load burden, permit holidays to be taken up, training courses and visits to be undergone. Planning for these predictable needs involves making assumptions as to their incidence, magnitude and importance such that greater contingency is probably always desirable but, of course, the inescapable constraint lies in the availability or scarcity of adequately qualified personnel.

Reflections on the foregoing

1 *The preoccupation with economics*
The contrast between the general acceptance of economic methodology and disinterest in human relations is stark indeed. It is surprising that given the economic frustrations which the United Kingdom has been suffering for some fifty years or more, this paradox has not received more attention. It may seem logical to attribute preoccupation with monetary theory, fiscal policy, anti-inflation demand regulation and the like to the relatively poor performance of the British economy but this argument is simplistic if only because policy and decisions are made by people, not by theory itself. But the aspect which needs to be emphasized is the habitual conscious application of economic analysis. 'Perhaps economic failure does inevitably result in a pre-occupation with economies and financial management but if this leads to a disinterest in operations or production management amounting to sheer ignorance and, in turn, to the accountant's emphasis on risk aversion as opposed to successful execution of properly evaluated risk enterprises, then the consequences will be very serious indeed.' Whatever the significance of policies, this imbalance clearly matters and it was with this view in mind that the Invergordon operational planning and execution was approached. There is no suggestion that any of the practices or actions described in the preceding chapter was entirely original or new. But the deliberate, calculated and comprehensive approach was unusual in its uniformity and in being concerted throughout. If this statement is regarded as questionable, consider to take only one example from the entire field of human relations, the abundant evidence to suggest that much personnel selection in industry is as haphazard, subjective, disorganized, aimless and ineffective as it was twenty years ago. The reader can well judge from personal experience – so much for the emphasis on manpower planning and utilization.

2 *The contrast at Invergordon*
Invergordon could have been used as a test-bed for innovations in human relations but, instead, it was decided to adopt as conservative approach to human relations as was the case with technological matters. This was not because of lack of imagina-

tion, ideas or appetite but because there was too much at stake to court project failure by adopting untried or unproved methods. However, many of the policies and practices actually adopted were unusual at the time and still are. Many have been sufficiently difficult to execute as to suggest that a more adventurous philosophy would have encountered very grave risks indeed. Much that was done failed to survive the pressures engendered by the onslaught of the oil-related industries from 1972 onwards. Equally survival itself might well have been even more difficult and costly had a less conservative approach prevailed. This remains as the central conclusion to be drawn from experience at Invergordon – management will underrate the extent and significance of deliberate and detailed attention to human relations at its peril, as will the rest of the community. There is abundant evidence to suggest that these perils abound more intensively in our industrial society than need be the case and if much remains to be learned in developing a better understanding of human behaviour, enough is already known to enable us to build a better society than that which now inhabits Scotland including the Highlands.

Bibliography

CMND 3819 *The Production of Primary Aluminium*, HMSO, 1968

DONOVAN, *Royal Commission on Trades Unions and Employers' Organizations*. HMSO, 1967

GOLD, P. A., *The Selection and Training of Foremen for a New Aluminium Smelter*, Imperial College, 1969

HANSARD, Statement in Parliament by the Board of Trade, HMSO, 24 July 1968

HERZBERG, HAUSNER, SNYDERMAN, *The Motivation to Work*, John Wiley & Sons Inc, 1959

LILIENTHAL, D., *TVA – Democracy on the March*, Harper & Row, 1943

MILLER and RICE, *Systems of Organization*, Tavistock, 1967

TAYLOR, *Shop Management*, Harper Bros, 1910

TURNER, R., *The Gove Alumina Project*, AIME, 1973

WOODWARD, PROFESSOR J., *Management and Technology*, HMSO. 1958

——, *Industrial Organization*, HMSO, 1965

Index